Letters From Lockdown

Elaine Farmer

In the middle of the journey of our life, I came to myself, in a dark wood, where the direct way was lost. It is a hard thing to speak of . . . but, in order to tell of the good that I found there, I must tell of the other things I saw there.

Danto, *Inferno* Canto I:1-60 *The Dark Wood and the Hill*

Letters From Lockdown

Friendship Going Viral

Elaine Farmer

Adelaide
2020

Cover art work: Garth Ryan
Cover design: Myf Cadwallader
Layout, in Minion Pro 11, by Extel Solutions, India.

ISBN   978-1-925679-88-5   soft
        978-1-925679-89-2   hard
        978-1-925679-90-8   epub
        978-1-925679-91-5   pdf

Published by:

An imprint of the ATF Press Publishing
Group owned by ATF (Australia) Ltd.
PO Box 234
Brompton, SA 5007
Australia
ABN 90 116 359 963
www.atfpress.com
Making a lasting impact

For Bill,
Our children, Julian and Catherine,
And all my other friends

Table of Contents

Introduction

I've always enjoyed letters. When I was a child it was very special to receive a letter, 'Miss Elaine Haigh' on the envelope, 'Dear Elaine' on the card or note. The 'Miss' made me feel grown-up. Letters usually arrived only for my parents; receiving a letter myself was definitely a 'for me?' moment.

Years later during our early diplomatic postings, long before the convenience and speed of computers and emails, I often filled hours writing letters to friends. In those days, the spouses (mostly wives) of diplomats were quite commonly not permitted to work by local labour laws so we were on our own in finding occupation, meaning and purpose. Writing letters seemed a good idea. I would write pages and pages, double-sided, thick letters that then needed extra postage! These letters kept me connected with home and friends. They provided occupation and I loved receiving replies.

One reply effected a considerable change in my thinking. A friend wrote saying she would always put my letters aside till a quiet moment when, with feet up and a cup of coffee or a glass of wine to hand, she would open it and enter another world. I came to realise the simple fact that receiving letters gave real pleasure to others, as well as to me. I noticed that, as letters continued to be exchanged, they became learning exercises. Titbits of information, gradual opening up of minds and hearts; slowly others revealed more and more of themselves. Their joys, sorrows, doubts and questions about life expanded their characters for me. In learning more about them, I was more able to give to them. And I grew as a result.

Over the years, I learned that what I could give in letters to my friends was more important than what I received in turn. This is what can happen with friends. They become safe places for each other.

Places where self-defensive shields can be put to one side, and the offering of friendship becomes an offering of the self. For me, this giving became a real form of hospitality, hospitality which offers the other that safe place where trust can grow and people can truly be themselves.

Hospitality was central to life with my husband Bill in diplomacy; the diplomat's table is where relationships are forged, friendships begun, and national interests tended. Through my letters, hospitality acquired centrality in a very different way but one which I think is no less valuable for its being quiet and mostly hidden.

Hospitality became even more alive when I was ordained an Anglican priest. It became the glue that kept the two parts of my identity—priest and ambassador's wife—together. Spiritual and material held as one. What I did in preparing diplomatic occasions is what I do when preparing the altar to celebrate the eucharist. I want the linen smooth, the flowers fresh, the candles trimmed, the silver polished. I want the music just right and every little detail attended to so guests at both table and altar can feel invited and welcome.

The letters in this book were written to friends during this 2020 coronavirus pandemic, a time when many friends seem farther away than during normal times. It is not a book about God. It is not a book about church or faith. But, if you are a person of faith, you will know God laughs and cries when we do—God is in the shadows in these letters as well as in the sunshine. If you are not a person of faith, I hope you will see in them life in all its exuberance, humour and sorrow. For it's the same thing, really; we're just using different words.

May I suggest that you brew some tea or coffee, or pour yourself a glass of wine, and settle down with me and my friends, think how you've coped in these COVID times, and enter another world.

> Who dare say No, when such is your request
> that each around your table should be guest,
> that here the ancient word should live as new,
> 'Take, eat and drink—all this is meant for you.'[1]

Elaine Farmer
October 2020

---

1. John Bell, Hymn No. 259 in *Together in Song. Australian Hymn Book II*, Harper Collins *Religious*, 1999, and reprinted 2005 with permission from *Wild Goose Songs 3, Love from Below*, Wild Goose Publications.

1
The Wars of the Roses

Dear Friends,

The Wars of the Roses are not over. At least not in my garden, where roses are rampaging through autumn. Experienced gardeners tell me that the summer bushfires filled the atmosphere with so much smoke that, when the rain came, gardens were showered with nutrients. I've no idea whether that's true or not but after my rose bushes were smashed by the hailstorm and drenched by rain they have come back blooming. It's as if they've wiggled their roots with delight and gone English on me, saying, "Cor, I do love a good summer prune!" The results have been astonishing. Great blousy blooms sending delirium amongst the bees and filling every vase I can find. Mind you, the bushes have also gone into major self-defence mode, producing the most vicious thorns, and there's been blood on the ground as I've tried to harvest their bounty. Worth bleeding for . . . we sit surrounded by bowls of beauty.

Apart from the roses, I'm over 2020!

So far this year we've had horrendous bushfires causing untold loss of lives, homes, livelihoods, livestock, forests, native animals and birds. Then floods and, at least in our part of Australia, The Hailstorm which smashed its way through cars, buildings and gardens. Now it's The Plague.

In recent times the big money seemed to be on whether we'd get frogs or boils after the fires, floods and hail but there wasn't much mention of plagues. I find the language intriguing. Another example of how the Bible has wormed its way into the English language and—were I a betting person—I'd bet most people who've been talking about raining frogs or bursting boils have no idea where their colourful images come from.

So now we are all more or less stuck. Hunkered down at home getting infuriated by overexcited journalists who persist in saying we are "bunkered" down. Travel curtailed (give or take a qualifying word here and there). Out-of-control citizenry rampaging through supermarkets buying every toilet roll in sight; this must be the first time in recorded history that loo paper has been the object of passionate desire. Hoarding on a scale not seen since World War II say those who remember those days and, no, I don't. I'm not that old. Businesses folding or as near as spit to doing so. Talking of which, we're all supposed to keep 1.5 metres apart; I can hear lots of little boys (and big ones for that matter) boldly declaring they can spit further than that. So much for social distancing. That's one of the new buzzwords.

While restaurants and cafes, for example, are closing around us some businesses are doing quite well. Traditional butchers are beaming over queues they've not seen since before giant supermarkets pushed their who-cares-about-quality-convenience-is-the-thing mantra on to a gullible marketplace. Homeware suppliers are reporting a 400% increase in sales of freezers. One major outfit says they could sell a thousand a day if they could get hold of them. Even plant nurseries are reporting a surge in requests for vegetable seedlings as people begin to remember that vegetables grow in the ground and once upon a time most people grew their own. They don't seem to remember that plants take time to grow, but then all signs indicate that we'll be confined to barracks for a very long time so maybe they will get to use their produce.

Then there's the whole obsession with hand sanitiser. Important, of course, but there's plenty of soap around, people, no shortage of water at the moment, and no need to panic. Sanitiser is completely unobtainable, as are the couple of simple ingredients to make it oneself. And on and on the madness goes with too many people becoming embarrassingly selfish and greedy. There have even been fights in the supermarket aisles with police called to haul the screaming combatants away, doubtless leaving behind plenty of other shoppers, their faces smug with virtue over their better behaviour, quietly stooping to pick up the coveted loo paper. Well, I hadn't really been going to buy any but . . .

Oh dear, I must beat back cynicism. I do understand that uncertainty is unsettling but it's extraordinary how many people seem unwilling to stop, think, and be rational. The virus might kill but common sense won't.

Meanwhile, Bill and I are well, comfortable and refusing to worry. We have cancelled travel to the US and the UK this year, a great disappointment as I was to have preached in several familiar and welcoming churches. The whole trip has become untenable, which is sad, but next year is another year and this year's dilemma will pass. The only thing worrying Bill right now is whether my mostly controlled obsessive (he says anal-retentive) tidiness will burst out, given all the time we will have at home rather than out and about. He, playing fast and loose with the German language, calls it my "Frau Kommandant" mode when I start cleaning or tidying him away. I deny it, of course, though I do admit that I did do something yesterday that I have never done. I cleaned the telephone hand pieces.

Then I did get over-enthusiastic as a gimlet eye lit upon my computer keyboard. Big mistake. I cleaned it and it is completely buggered, as we say in polite society. Or may be. I am told its inner workings may dry out. Twitching slightly with separation syndrome over threatened access to my computer, I took myself off into the allegedly plague-infected world to buy a replacement. Now I'm a bit like those butchers. Grinning. Not only were there plenty available but I bought one for only $A8.88. That's $A8.88! I suggested to the shop assistant that surely it must be $A88.88 but she just smiled and said I should leave quickly. I am still bemused. Anxiety allayed, this keyboard is pretty clunky—what else could it be at that price?—but it'll do for the moment.

While I was having that boring little adventure, Bill decided he'd try to repair the black wooden ducks in the garden that had been smashed by the hailstorm. Some years back a gardening magazine had said model black birds deter real birds from plopping on outdoor furniture. It proved to be true, to our astonishment. When we removed the broken bodies after the recent hailstorm we watched and waited. And, lo! the next morning, bird droppings. I kid you not. Now with super glue and spray paint, two are back on the job, albeit one is rather pigeon-toed, poor thing. Half a foot has gone missing but at least it's standing.

In all the anxiety being expressed about isolation a recurrent wail is "what will we do at home alone". It's another mantra of the moment. I imagine the introvert's reaction to social distancing might be, "who cares? I've been preparing for this all my life!" But another response, surely, is "read a book". Articles are appearing in the papers here to that effect, with some interesting suggestions from writers about their favourites. The classics might almost come back in fashion given the way they are currently being pushed. Bill and I are setting ourselves various projects to use our time in a focussed way. Apart from which, it's wonderful to be able to while away hours "just reading"; and be guilt-free! (Actually, I rarely feel guilty over reading!)

And, as a person who believes in living ritualistically—marking moments with meaning—I find myself remembering with pleasure my mother changing for the evening, donning high heels and lipstick, drawing that happy line between the working days and pleasurable evenings. As an 'old polio', I may not be able to do the high heel thing, but swanning round in a long dress and lipstick, lighting some candles, and reclining among the sofa cushions with a gin-and-tonic in hand is a fine way to fend off the doomsayers of our current world.

Stay well. Stay safe.

With love to you all,

Elaine
23 March 2020

2
One Fine Day

Dear Friends,

I saw the bottom of the ironing bin this week. It wasn't at all interesting and I hid it immediately with things I didn't feel like ironing. It's always the same. Necessity and discipline take me and my iron a good distance but discipline fades first. I decide I can wear something else and that's it for that session. I have to say that this week's assault on my crumpled belongings wasn't really much of an archaeological dig. There were a couple of "oh-I-wondered-where-that-was" moments but no treasures discovered. In days long gone, when our children were little and life was a rush and we'd be moving around from posting to posting, I had one rule about the ironing basket. When packing-up time came anything discovered unironed and lurking at the bottom was ditched. I figured if I hadn't noticed for a couple of years it obviously wasn't a treasure and we didn't need it.

In a rush of blood to the head and more over-enthusiasm, yesterday afternoon I thought it might be the moment to clean the fridge. I have survived. In fact, it wasn't too bad, the odd spill here and there but nothing insanitary. Little piles of unidentifiable crumbs but what harm could they be? As a granddaughter once said to me as she thrust a cicada shell in my face, "Don't worry, Granny, it's dead"! So I took everything out and happily found no mysteries gently mouldering in back corners. On the other hand, there was one mystery. I removed all the various shelves and bins but one defied me. I couldn't shift it and there was no sign of anything having dried into a gluey mass to stick the thing in place. One end moved; the other wouldn't. Then the discovery: a piece of tape holding the bin to the door. "Ah," I thought. "That must be the original packing tape." Who would have thought? And why am I confessing?

Oh well, I have a clean fridge and a clean kitchen floor because I spilled so much water I had to do that job as well. It has to be said that, while it is easy to put these jobs off (and despite the packing tape I do clean the fridge!), it's very satisfying when they're done. Piles of neatly folded clothes and orderly wardrobes. It's called Virtue and it's matched only by admiring the gleam of freshly polished silver. Or getting up at 5.30am to go to the gym. The bliss-of-the-now for me at least is that gyms are closed. Too bad, so sad, but I am exercising at home and I love alarm-free mornings.

These activities haven't taken up much time this week, and certainly haven't been allowed to get between me a good book. I must tell you of this week's discovery. Bill and I are trying (and failing) to reduce our book collection by idly reading this and that and deciding what we don't want to read again. Bill is much better at being tough. I tend to read with a pencil and Post-it notes and am totally undisciplined about what I Just Must Keep! I've had a lovely time this week with a book published in 1947 (and republished by Virago in 1985) called *One Fine Day*. It's written by an English novelist and writer of wartime essays for *The New Yorker*, with the deliciously evocative name of Mollie Panter-Downes. Could she be anything but English with that name! As I've read her book, she has become for me 'Miss Mollie'. 'Miss Panter-Downes' is a bore to keep typing and repetition makes it somehow stuffy. 'Ms' just doesn't suit her, or her book; it's far too anachronistic and thin-lipped. She was married to one Clare Robinson but, with great respect to him and his ancestry, why would she call herself 'Robinson' when she could swan through life with her own delightful handle?

One Fine Day is set in the English countryside in 1946. The Second World War had swept away one world but whatever brave new world would take its place was still unclear. "The past . . . was pressed like a dry butterfly between the glass of Edwardian photograph frames," she writes; now uncertainty, grim realities, nostalgia and bravery stamped themselves on village lives. The novel revolves around the particular struggles of Laura, a middle-class woman born to a well-mannered world of servants and leisure, suddenly struggling with cleaning, cooking and an enormous garden. Both house and garden defeat her; her husband is polite and tries to be helpful and not peevish but the disorderly nature of this new world unsettles him and he flees daily to his work in London.

There is no particular story and its characters, though sharply drawn, are not explored. *One Fine Day* follows a theme, a set of reflections, rather than a series of events. It's beautifully written, lyrical, more like poetry than prose. "True is it that we have seen better days" from Shakespeare's *As You Like It* is the opening epigram and this thought pervades the whole book. Laura's husband Stephen reflects silently: "All his life he had expected to find doors opened if he rang, to wake up to the soft rattle of curtain rings being drawn back, to find the fires bright and the coffee smoking hot every morning as though household spirits had been working while he slept. And now the strings had been dropped, they all lay helpless as abandoned marionettes with nobody to twitch them". I hear Bill sighing empathetically.

This is an elegant and gentle book; sadness, loss and longing float from its pages. I found myself drawn into the story and sad for all who now find their worlds obliterated and who struggle to recreate their very selves. Though set in different times, *One Fine Day* is a book for this time of uncertainty, sadness and loss, with its tinge of knowledge that nothing will ever be quite the same again. How we came to have Miss Mollie's book is a mystery but no way is she going anywhere but back on our bookshelves, where I hope she will rest comfortably until I take her out again to lose myself in a vanished world. I hope she will be joined on my shelves by more of her work. I'm now in the market for her *Letters from London,* and also *The Shoreless Sea* which was hugely popular all those long years ago. Do we need to buy more books? Well no, but there are worse obsessions. I grew up in a house laden with books. Reading was central to life. The family all reading and no sound but the ticking of the clock and my father crunching on boiled lollies. And I remember my mother used to warn against complaining about dusty bookshelves. "If I go to dust and put my glasses on to see what I'm doing," she would say, "I'll simply find something I must read and that'll be that." Wise woman.

Enjoy reading. Stay well. Stay safe.

With love to you all,

Elaine
30 March 2020

3
Sabbath Days

Dear Friends,

Once upon a time, a crowd was a crowd and we all knew what that meant. Then in these strange times, a crowd became three and the world was a whole new place. Now, as if we are not already sufficiently discombobulated (lovely chewy word I use whenever I can), a crowd has become two.

In those lost times when a crowd was still three, we invited friends to visit, one at a time on different days. They would arrive bearing their own wine glass, the side garden gate open for them to come through to the back garden and take a seat at one end of our outside table. We'd provide champagne and sit at the other end of the table, all of us carefully observing social distancing requirements. It felt rather jolly, with a frisson of mild excitement over something different and that aren't-we-managing-well-in-adverse-times feeling.

Louise was our last visitor and arrived, not just with her wine glass, but bearing a basket with scones wrapped in a towel and hot from her oven, butter, bowls of jam and cream, and favourite pretty china plates. "Just because it's the end of the world doesn't mean we can't have beautiful stuff", she said, paraphrasing, she tells me, the director of *Mad Max: Fury Road*. How right that is. We opened the champagne—"nothing goes better with scones, jam and cream than champagne" said Louise—and chatted and gossiped and toasted all our friends, especially those far from us, not least those of you in New York and Indonesia, England and New Zealand, all places where we have spent so much time and acquired so many friends. We hold you close to our hearts.

The day after Louise's visit a crowd became two and our tiny fun gatherings were over. Bill and I apparently constitute a crowd. It's as well we have separate studies in different parts of the house or one or other of us would begin to find the crowd-as-two definition one too many. We have just spent what seems like half a day trying to set up Zoom and get computer microphones working. Somehow we failed and tense words flew back and forth. What we did wrong remains a mystery. We are now skulking in our own studies, shiny with virtue and both convinced the other was wrong. This too, like the coronavirus, will pass. Everyone says getting Zoom is SO easy. Now they're talking about party apps and videos and The Dear knows what else about how we can communicate. I was doing that already. Communicating, I mean. Actually, I admit Zoom will be fun once we've ironed out the kinks but, please, not all day! I can feel a sense of frustration rising because it's all such an interruption!

I've been having a much lovelier time (pretty much anything would be lovelier than struggling with computers) this week re-reading an old favourite. Mollie Panter-Downes' *One Fine Day* that I talked about last week sent me on a hunt for my copy of *Ex Libris: Confessions of a Common Reader* by Anne Fadiman. It's a 1998 book of essays about books and reading and I think the somewhat episodic nature of *One Fine Day* reminded me of Fadiman's essays. I enjoy essays, probably because I had a profound respect for this literary form instilled in me at high school. We studied Francis Bacon and were told that it takes a very particular skill to write with such a 'beautiful economy of words'. The point stuck. It's a skill I haven't acquired, I'm afraid, but maybe I remembered because I could do with a finger in the back, to keep trying.

Fadiman's book is simply lovely. I haven't finished this re-read yet. I'm savouring it, spinning it out essay by essay. I feel like that American professor of literature who hadn't read all Jane Austen because he couldn't bear the thought of life without one of her books to read for the first time. On the other hand, instead of starting at the beginning, I couldn't resist searching for the wonderful essay about her family's obsessive proofreading habit. She describes them reading the menu at a restaurant:

> "They've transposed the *e* and the *i* in Madeira sauce," commented my brother.

"They've made Bel Paese into one word," I said, "and it's lowercase."

"At least they spell better than the place where we had dinner last Tuesday," said my mother. "*They* serve P-E-A-K-I-N-G duck."

It could be Bill and me. We were shopping once and I found a red marker pen in the basket. "We don't need this," I said. "I know," Bill answered, "but I had to correct one of the advertisements." I understood. I've done that to restaurant menus. Bad form, I know, but sometimes one is driven. As one once was in a seafood restaurant offering crap and lobster.

Fadiman has me saying "yes, yes", or laughing, or even getting a lump in the throat. "Books wrote our life story," she says, "and as they accumulated on our shelves (and on our windowsills, and underneath our sofa, and on top of our refrigerator), they became chapters in it themselves. How could it be otherwise?" How indeed. When I was growing up the only room that didn't have bookshelves was the bathroom.

Fadiman writes about how she and her husband merged their libraries some years after they married. Somehow they did that without (according to her account) too much acrimony. Bill's just finished completely sorting and rearranging our books. I kept out of it. (More virtue.) I knew the whole thing would end in tears and not even before bedtime if I tried to share in the job. Now English literature, that is books by UK English writers, are in one place; Australian elsewhere. Autobiographies have their own case; ditto biographies. Literature from other countries' authors is shelved in splendid isolation and so is everything about war. Really? A whole case on war? Books on politics of all sorts huddle together in Bill's study and theology in mine though I have quietly and surreptitiously spilled over into another room. Shhhh.

Back to Anne Fadiman . . . I can't decide whether I fit her "carnal love" or "courtly love" variety of book lovers. The latter fits more with the way I was brought up with rigid training in, for example, carefully turning pages *only from the top corner,* holding a book carefully without straining its spine and never, NEVER placing it upside down with the pages open. I commit this last sin all the time, I'm afraid! And I stick Post-it notes on pages and make pencil markings and comments, though I am picky about which books I so defile. On the other hand, something in me recoils with horror when I see Bill ripping chapters out of books and throwing them away when he's read them. This is, I grant, only with paperbacks of the unimportant and cheaply replaceable variety and only when we're travelling. Bill says it simply makes things lighter when he's recumbent. Anne Fadiman's father did the same thing unencumbered by guilt and, according to his daughter, with nonchalance, so I suppose that's respectable precedent.

I very much enjoyed Fadiman's account of her teenage production of sonnets and rude awakening when her ninth-grade effort was not picked out as among the best to be displayed to her class. She recalls dismay because her teacher Miss Farrer's favourite "was about the Acropolis. Twenty-eight years later, I still remember its author called the Parthenon 'a ruined Crown'. It never occurred to me that this metaphor alone was worth a hundred of my sonnets". Fadiman looks back and sees herself, not as a soul who could have produced such a poetic idea, but as "a priggish little pedant who would no more have permitted a rogue trochee to sneak among her perfect iambs than show up in Miss Farrer's class with a smudge on her monogrammed school uniform". I like her honesty and her whimsical style. I am also deeply relieved that my teenage efforts have sunk without trace. I hope. If you haven't read *Ex Libris* do seek it out. I hope you enjoy it as much as I do.

Speaking of writing, and returning to the troubled world we live in, I've had a letter today from a dear friend, Susan, an extremely talented Episcopal Church priest in the US. Susan muses on the familiar phrase 'a month of Sundays', and of how we ought not be influenced by its traditional implication of an interminably dreary time. Instead, she recalls the meaning of Sabbath as a time apart, not for feeling bored and dreary, but to be used as

> a time of restoration and renewal—the unexpected gift of time to reconnect with friends for which there never seemed to be enough time, to return to unfinished projects abandoned by the press of more immediate tasks, and, finally, to revive an interest, an idea, an intention always deferred to 'not now . . . later when I have more time'.

Susan is right, and her letter was timely, arriving as it did on Palm Sunday, the beginning of the most holy week in the Christian calendar. Some of you might want to stop reading at such a mention but I hope you read on—you might just miss something if you don't! Holy Week is a confronting week. It brings us to the heart of Christian faith. That heart is marked by horror and blessing, improbabilities, profoundly meaningful metaphors, and a demand that we balance all this by trying to see how the ghastliness of crucifixion and the blessing of resurrection work in each of our lives. It's less about wondering whether Jesus's tomb really was empty and more about whether we lock ourselves into empty tombs in our lives, those things which prevent us from being the best we can be—for our own sakes, and for those around us.

Susan suggests we make "Sabbath time" of all this time we now have in isolation. It's an excellent suggestion and an excellent term. It wraps all our efforts to be kind to each other, to keep in touch, to keep smiling, and to live in hope, with purpose and focus.

I wish you all joy in embracing Sabbath time. You might also keep in mind what another of my friends, Robbie, has said to me: "Big earrings! Every evening I put on big earrings!" Earrings may not be your thing but embrace the spirit!

With love

Elaine
6 April 2020

4
Easter Greetings

Dear Friends,

Good Friday

I woke on Good Friday to a grey leaden sky which was weeping softly. We have had good rains in recent weeks, rain which was so needed after the horrendous summer Australia has endured, and brown has turned to green around us. Any rain is always a blessing in this land but it was Good Friday and there are always tears in the shadow of blessings, and so the skies wept.

It's been a tough week. And not just because it was Holy Week; that's always a challenge. There's been the continuing sad news about the horrifying situation in the United Kingdom and the United States, particularly in New York. There was the shock of the British Prime Minister's being taken to hospital and intensive care. There has been drama after drama over the variety of problems people have encountered in quarantine, isolation and social lockdown. In Australia, we've had some 2500 passengers on a cruise ship allowed to disembark without proper checking, hence bearing the coronavirus— and death—hither and yon. A former colleague of Bill's reports that three of her contacts in Indonesia are dead. A friend in the US reports a sick colleague in his own office. Our Ambassador to Indonesia has been flown back to Australia for medical reasons and only skeleton staffs remain in the various places where Australia is represented in that country.

As I looked out at the rain, my mind turned to those trying valiantly to stem the pandemic. To the politicians struggling to juggle so many urgent but irreconcilable needs. To the scientists laboriously testing and experimenting, making their way painstakingly and meticulously through myriad possibilities to create a vaccine. I thought about the film footage I saw last week of young doctors, hurriedly being graduated so they could join the fight to try to save lives. Fresh eager young faces, warriors in this battle. How many of them will die in the process, losing their places in the future of the world? I thought of the young about-to-be nurse who has lost his casual jobs, therefore his income, and cannot get to his last classes to qualify so he, too, can care for the sick and the dying.

And I wondered, what will be the impact on these brave young souls? What could possibly have prepared them for the stark moment when they might have to make a decision—that this person will live, and that person die? Probably, the answer is—nothing. And they might have to face this decision over and over. Sophie's Choice. I looked at their bright eyes as they took their Hippocratic Oath to maintain the highest of medical ethics and I grieved for them, fearing how soon those bright eyes might dim, with distress over their patients, with fear for themselves, and with shock over their inability to make their idealism save the world. For those who survive, how long will they carry the scars of this experience, and how will they manage? Probably, the answer is—always, and with courage. I pray for them.

But there has been good news. In Australia at least, drops in numbers of infections, even though they are slight falls and we are all warned to continue vigilance. Friends of ours who have been in isolation or quarantine are now free and well. A friend in New York who has been sick has recovered and did not have COVID-19. And a friend here in Canberra who did contract the disease has recovered and is out of quarantine. And how did Howard get the disease? Well, he was in London on business, there was a dinner party, and the guests included the British Prime Minister, the Prince of Wales and Prince Albert of Monaco. Intriguing thought. Were the monarchists trying to knock off the Australian republican, or was it the other way round? We need all the laughs we can get at this difficult time. And Howard can claim bragging rights over this!

Holy Saturday

On Saturday I woke to a blue sky and bracing winds. It was as if the winds were driving the shadows away along with the rain. As if Easter brightness had come a day early, because Holy Saturday is the in-between time, the dead day. We were in limbo and the bleakness of Good Friday had not yet disappeared on the wind. The resurrection hope of Easter was still a glow on a far horizon. Which is as it always is. Good Friday might well trade in death, and Easter in life, but we don't get one without the other. The two have always wandered through every life, hand in hand, though we might sometimes wish it were not so. But it is. That's life; so be it. But the other side of Good Friday is hope, not easy for many to see, with that day's powerful pictures of blood and death. Strange story it is, but lovely, and one that lives at the heart of life in its beauty and its tragedy.

Easter Day

"This is the day that the Lord has made. Let us be glad and rejoice in it." Every Easter Day countless preachers begin their sermons with these words. "Christ is risen! Hallelujah!" And there is joy, and relief, and bright light after the darkness, and bells ring, and anthems of thanksgiving are sung. The long Lenten journey of self-examination and facing the worst of which humankind is capable—symbolised by the crucifixion of Jesus—is over for another year. The time has arrived when we can once more relish the hope and new life born on the cross.

How? Why? What on earth was it that made Mary Magdalene and the other women, and, eventually, the disciples, believe that Jesus had risen from the dead? How could they believe the impossible, accept the improbable, everything they knew was simply unacceptable, unrealistic? Nothing in real life, theirs or ours, can explain accepting such a thing as the resurrection of the dead, a thing of legends. There is no evidence, no proof, but then it isn't about evidence or proof. It's about mystery.

Those ancients accepted something they saw in their history as a nation, as a community. Sitting around campfires, and in the storytelling of their childhoods, generation after generation, these people had learned the tales of their history. They remembered their parents telling of slavery in Egypt, of hard-won freedom, of wandering in the desert wilderness, and of learning about the wilderness of the soul. A history of disasters and countless endings. Destruction. Death. Loss of hope. They remembered being taught that the one steady and unchanging thing that had supported their ancestors was their belief that, no matter how tumultuous the times had been, their God supported them, was faithful to them—and they had survived. It was an extraordinary belief.

Now they were living in new brutal and dangerous times, in new oppression under the Romans. And some of them believed they saw the same grace and divine faithfulness in Jesus, a man like them, now, it seemed, risen from the dead for his grave was empty. In faith, they believed. It was an extraordinary belief.

Many of you may not have read this far. Many of you will not see the relevance of ancient tales to our own times, our own lives. Many of you will not be interested in this thing called resurrection that we celebrate this day, the faith that supports it and the hope that is its guiding light. But (if you are still reading) consider this. There is something for us to learn in the experience of these ancestors. In understanding our lives and our world, we need perhaps to begin in the same place they did—with the endings. With the dreams that have died. The hopes that have withered. The deaths we have mourned. The ones we have buried. The elderly parents. The friends. The dead babies. All the loved and lost ones for whom some of us have prayed that the story of this day is true—and live in hope.

It's a challenge, this resurrection faith, resurrection hope. It's testing. Sadly none of this makes sense to many people today, and maybe it doesn't to you either. But I recommend you give it a passing thought. There are no proofs. There is no evidence. But there is mystery and wonder, and we will find exactly that when we look into the eyes of those around us and see the best of which we are created. Think of those young doctors, and the young nurse. Think of all the people working tirelessly for nothing more than a smile and know you are looking into the eyes of the Risen Christ.

Grace and Peace be with you all this Easter, and always. We have survived the summer, we will survive this pandemic too.

Keep safe and don't give up on hope.

With love as always

Elaine
13 April 2020

5
Old Scones

Dear Friends,

During this pandemic everyone is talking about getting domestic jobs done. While it is a good opportunity for that sort of catch-up, I've also found it a spur to apply a bit of discipline in other areas. I've actually managed to do a decent amount of serious writing. Bill, a fading Latinist, says I should branch out into poetry, producing *COVID's Amores*. I ignore this.

That being said, I cleaned out the pantry this week. It's one of those jobs which, once started, you have to finish because there's so much disarray created. Even so, abandonment lurked dangerously in the wings along with thoughts of something better to do like sit in the autumn sun with a good book. But two things kept me going: mystery; and re-imposing order, which is the joy of any anal-retentive obsessive nerd's heart. I even attacked drawers and created beautiful order. Plates in their proper piles; mugs and jugs now on military parade, handles all lined up. I sighed with pleasure, only to note the wickedness of Bill's grin when he saw my handiwork. I know he will surreptitiously poke a handle out of alignment. Then I'll straighten it and he'll mess it up again and this will go on till one of us gets bored. Which is quickly.

Such fun I had, sniffing this spice, tasting that, and merrily chucking what had already gone to God. Labelling the lids of all the spice containers and happily lining them up in their own drawer. Heaven! And then—The Discovery. Huddled in a back corner minding its own business behind tinned tomatoes and long-life milk was the morning's mystery. A packet of scone mix. Scone mix? Why would I have that? It is a truth universally acknowledged that I don't bake. I could only think it must have been for a cooking session with grandchildren but I knew if ever I'd planned to teach them to make scones I'd have started from scratch. Both my daughter and my daughter-in-law are good bakers who would never use a packaged mix and I'd always have to try to match their high standards. None of this nonsense of buying packaged stuff full of chemicals for them—or for me. I sniffed huffily.

Unable to solve this mystery I decided (perhaps rashly) that I might as well use this scone mix. This would be the day for Bill and me to go to the movies. 'Going to the pictures' was the term when we were children, or even 'going to the flicks'. In this time of social lockdown going to the movies means at home and definitely during the day. It has to be during the day because that's work time and therefore sitting down to watch a movie has a frisson of naughtiness about it. So that afternoon Bill chose a movie and I baked scones, got out the best china and jam spoons, filled pretty bowls with jams and thick cream, made tea. We drew the blinds and settled down to our feast.

Can I tell you that, though I don't bake, these scones were pretty well everything a scone should be? Baking perfection! Light and tasty. Just the right amount of flouriness. I was inordinately pleased with myself. There was just one tiny matter we'd discovered that didn't solve the mystery as to why I had packet scone mix but did explain why I'd forgotten it was there. The use-by date was 31 July 2013.

We are both well and alive and enjoyed a huge laugh. We thought of John Malkovich in *Red Two*. Do you remember the scene? He, Bruce Willis and Mary-Louise Parker entered a Moscow apartment that had been sealed for forty years. Malkovich picked up a chocolate Wagon Wheel and started to eat it. His companions were aghast but he said, all innocence, "but this was made before use-by dates were invented; there's no use-by date on it!"

We had a use-by date but I'd figured nothing much could go wrong with a sealed packet of flour and baking powder. Not even a weevil could have got at it. It's the same sort of thing we felt back in the late eighties when we found three large out-of-date jars of Vegemite in a cupboard in the Embassy residence in Mexico City. Vegemite, for those of you who aren't familiar with this Australian delicacy, is a salty, indeed very salty, spread made out of leftover yeast extract, in itself a waste by-product of beer manufacture. Nice! Was the time most Australian babies were weaned on the stuff via a smear on a crust when they were teething. President Obama declared it "horrible", but with a smile.

Given that the bottles of Vegemite were out-of-date by years, we decided they hadn't been left by our immediate predecessor. What's the harm, we thought? Actually, I think it would be difficult (a) for Vegemite to go off, and (b) to tell if it had. I doubt we got through all the "health food of a nation", as it's been called, during our two and a half years in Mexico so we probably left some (a lot) for our successors. It may still be in the residence. I have no idea.

Leftovers are a part of diplomatic life anyway. And that includes pets. In Mexico, we also inherited a HUGE female Great Dane called Xotchil from our predecessor, and eventually we passed on our two American cocker spaniels to US Ambassador John Negroponte. Pets, sadly, have use-by dates.

Equally sadly, alcohol does not. In many places over forty years of diplomatic wandering we inherited a startling array of opened and half-used bottles of alcohol. We have sipped and tasted our way through a quite bizarre (to us) range of liqueurs, for example. People rarely ask for stickies, or even brandy, nowadays but, once upon a time, the range of drinks offered guests was wide, with various spirits before dinner, wines with, and liqueurs after. It was standard practice after dinner for a tray with six or eight bottles to be carried around to choose from. So we sampled the leftovers we found in each residence and I'm quite sure left behind many of our own. Including things we'd inherited but didn't like. And so the alcoholic merry-go-round spins and spins. All over the world there are bottles languishing on dusty shelves feeling unloved and unwanted, like abandoned toys in a children's nursery, just waiting for someone to savour them again. Blue Curaçao eat your heart out.

Meanwhile, here in Canberra, as I fiercely guard my newly tidy shelves and drawers, I have pointed out to Bill that 'use-by' date can have quite a wide application. I have also hinted unkindly at the applicability of 'best before'.

For something completely different . . . next Saturday 25 April is ANZAC Day. ANZAC for Australian and New Zealand Army Corps. The equivalent of the British Remembrance Day and the American Memorial Day, it is the day Australians and New Zealanders honour the memory of our war dead, military and civilian. While war fosters hate and kills millions there is one thing it cannot kill: human need to love and be loved. Next Saturday is also the day two dear friends, Carol and Peter, were to have been married at the Little Church Around the

Corner in New York. Now that will not be their wedding day. But we can still drink champagne and Bill and I will raise our glasses on Saturday to them, to their future, and to love. This pandemic will end. There will be a future—and another wedding day.

Let me leave you with an amusing and brief line sent by a friend this week. A priest, a monk and a rabbit went into a pub together. The rabbit said "I think I'm a spelling mistake".

On that crazy note, have a good week keeping very, very safe.

With love

Elaine
20 April 2020

6
Mixed Memories

Dear Friends,

ANZAC Day, the day which has morphed into Australia's 'secular sacred' day. Established initially to honour lives lost at the disastrous campaign in Gallipoli in Turkey in 1915, it is now held in memory of lives, Australian and New Zealand in particular, lost in all wars. A sobering statistic used during this year's commentary was that, per head of population, Australia lost more soldiers in World War I than any other nation.

Usually on ANZAC Day, services are held at dawn, and marches and solemn ceremonies later in the morning, in cities and towns across Australia. But 2020 is not a normal year. Coronavirus and social distancing rule. No marches. Only the barest of ceremonies. Wreaths laid. The Last Post played. This year many of us got up before dawn and stood in our driveways, on balconies, in open paddocks, turned our radios or phones up, placed candles on the ground, and listened to the Last Post floating into the dawn. Many families gathered and it was touching to watch, on the news, young children playing the Last Post on bugles or trumpets, and knowing they had solemnly practised and practised for this moment. One of our neighbours walked round our block during the morning, playing a lament on his bagpipes, his little children following him beating makeshift drums. Bill and I rose early, I cut rosemary for remembrance from the garden, and we too stood in our driveway to remember.

During the past week I talked with two of my friends about ANZAC Day. We are more or less the same generation, our fathers were all veterans, and none of us finds this an easy day. We remember the 1960s and Australian playwright Alan Seymour's controversial play *The One Day of the Year*. Banned at one stage for fear its provocative critique of ANZAC Day and the traditions surrounding it would offend old soldiers. There was little in it at all about war; it was more about attitudes and generational clashes and questioning how a day that many saw as just beer-swilling and two-up, an illegal betting game, could legitimately hold a whole nation in thrall.

My friends and I remember that critique and it coloured our thinking about this day. Now, while honouring the best of ANZAC Day's meaning and intention, we remain disturbed by a mixture of things: the desire to honour sacrifice and the great gift of lives lost in a good cause too often diving into great pools of sentimentality; the tendency to use the easy shorthand of 'soldiers'—as I also am doing here—pushing out of the balance, navy and air force; the tendency to wax lyrical about defence forces, pushing out of focus the terrible civilian casualties of war; the tendency, perhaps easing slightly, to forget the sacrifices of families, in wartime enduring constant privations and, when hostilities were over, years of living with damaged returned servicemen, minds too often shattered by things no-one should ever see, hearing things no-one should ever hear, and unable to do anything but endure. No counselling then. No recognition of crippling grief. No realisation of Post-Traumatic Stress Disorder. Just get on with your life and forget.

They couldn't. My father was one of those damaged men. He tried to get on with it but the effort turned into rage and irrationality that loomed over our family for all of our childhood, and beyond. The story of damaged families like mine is the dark underbelly of ANZAC Day. My friends and I remember this day as sad, gloomy and tense. More even than all other days we crept round quietly, keeping to ourselves, asking no questions, fearing the emotional rage that could break out into punishments and tears.

ANZAC Day is therefore a day of mixed memories. It is easy to understand and accept the desire to remember and give honour but oh! so easy to see how we get it out of kilter. It will always be so because we human beings are such a mess of emotions and, in meaning well, we often ring bells of celebration that clunk just a bit off-key. Which means, I think, it's up to us to think ourselves into a different space. No way did all those servicemen (and women in more recent times) put their lives on the line, and too often lose them, so that life could not be lived, and lived to the full. They did not die for gloom, but for future and for peace. And they died for joy.

So we invited a friend for ANZAC Day lunch, dutifully keeping our distance from each other. Under Canberra's isolation rules we are now allowed up to two people at our house, preferably in the context of 'caring'. So Louise was caring for us and we for her! Coronavirus has bullied its way into the heart of Louise's life as travel bans have grounded her here while her partner is in Copenhagen. It was a glorious autumn day, all blue sky and bright sun. We sat in the garden and lunched on home-smoked salmon (courtesy of another friend, Ada, who goes to incredible lengths in cooking, as in making her own bread and sausages, and smoking salmon, trout and chicken). We savoured wonderful runny cheeses, and piles of fresh berries. We drank champagne, toasting servicemen and women, past and present, our veteran fathers, and Carol and Peter in New York who on Saturday were celebrating their 'non-wedding day' with champagne, roses and poetry. And we laughed.

A peak moment of our lunch came when Louise produced a tin of her homemade ANZAC Biscuits. They are a much-loved part of Australian culture. A homely mix of rolled oats, coconut, flour, butter and golden syrup. Some say they were developed during World War I by Australian women to send to the troops; some say they were developed by the troops themselves. My mother used to make them regularly and hers are a comfortable childhood memory. Too often now these biscuits are hard and dry—but not Mother's. And not Louise's. For the first time in decades here was the real thing: ANZACS, soft, bendy, buttery and sweet. Magic! Where had this recipe come from? A 1950s cookery book from Queensland. My mother was a Queenslander, like Louise, so maybe that great State should receive bouquets for producing Proper ANZAC Biscuits. By the way, all contrary opinions about these biscuits will not be received. With respect, of course.

Naturally I begged for the recipe, non-baker though I am, but I think I will have to make an effort each ANZAC Day to make these treasures my Mother made as she did her best to care for her damaged husband.

Some of you have written during the week asking what movie we watched over those scones the other day. Oh dear. I wish I could say that it was the latest, highly acclaimed, arty-farty award-winner that the WHOLE WORLD is raving about and that it was the wonder of the Senegal Film Festival or wherever, but that'd be a lie. It was

Carry On Up the Khyber, a movie of somewhat slight moment, and of even greater antiquity than the scone mix. It was one of a series of British movies from the 1960s and 70s that were enormously popular, though they may never have made it to the US. Comedies featuring such perennials as Sid James, Kenneth Williams and Joan Sims, all of them called *Carry On* whatever, and all of them dependent on bawdy jokes, *double entendre* and harmless smut. *Carry On Up the Khyber* was the best of them.

Speaking of ANZAC biscuits and baking, an amusing joke popped up this week, appropriately, given the day, sent by our friend Richard in New Zealand. An elderly and very sick man was lying in bed when a wonderful enticing aroma wafted into his bedroom. With great difficulty, he got out of bed and made his laborious way to the nearby kitchen where he saw a rack of freshly baked ANZAC Biscuits. He reached out a trembling hand to take one when his wife appeared, smacked his wrist and said sharply, "Leave them alone. They're for the funeral!"

On that note, I'll leave you for another week. Keep safe and keep well.

With love

Elaine
27 April 2020

7
Cocktails Anyone?

Dear Friends,

Apparently not every business is under savage assault in this coronavirus era. Here in Australia, home deliveries of pretty well everything are in high demand. Suppliers of specialised food items to high-end restaurants, the latter now all closed unless they've morphed into offering takeaway foods, are also moving into different retail areas. Direct sales are now going to anyone with a heap of money to pay for items normally unavailable on the open market or sold overseas only. I've never heard of Mottonai lamb, for example, but now the breeder has made over $A22,000 in ten days of home deliveries. The come-on of lower prices is a neat ploy to make the usually unattainable irresistible despite a still-high price tag. Fancy some Mooloolaba tuna normally costing $A70-80 per kilo and sold only at a fish market? It's going for a song at $A35 or so. How about $A150 per kilo for some steak usually exclusive to one Sydney restaurant? These suppliers might have taken an initial blow and had to completely re-organise their businesses but, even at these lower prices, they are apparently doing well. Bill and I aren't among those hanging on the telephone to place an order.

The other area going gangbusters is, not surprisingly, alcohol. The summer bushfires destroyed hope of good wine harvests, or any, in some areas this year but there are still plenty of supplies and demand is through the roof, we're told. I'm not sure whether some people think they can drown the virus internally, though admittedly the attempt would be less lethal then swallowing disinfectant. (Or injecting it! What was he—you know who I mean—thinking?) Still, alcohol seems to be the go-to comfort of the moment and many a household is indulging, if not in parties with friends and family, then in their own cocktail hours.

Why do we still talk about 'the cocktail hour' when people don't drink cocktails as they once did? Perhaps they do in the US, home of cocktails; you can let me know. Professor Google tells me the word 'cocktail' first appeared in an upstate New York newspaper in 1806, which rather questions the claims of New Orleans and of one Antoine Peychaud, an apothecary who opened his shop in the 1830s, that his mix of cognac, sugar, water and bitters was the original cocktail. I'll leave those of you who are American to fight it out among yourselves as to which claim is correct!

I don't drink cocktails except margaritas, a taste nurtured during our Mexican days. I tasted a dry martini once but didn't like it; Bill likes one occasionally. The first ever cocktail I tasted was in New York when I was in my extremely ignorant very early twenties. We were with a group of people at a Japanese restaurant, so seated on cushions on the floor, our legs dangling in a pit under the table. I was served a cocktail called Perfect Love (or was it a Geisha Girl?), a pale violet liquid with a maraschino cherry, and dry ice sending misty clouds sailing above the glass. Very pretty and a much more attractive sight than my labouring to get up afterwards. In my own defence, let me say that the little matter of having had polio rather knocks dreams of elegance out from under you. So getting up out of that sunken pit was never going to be a polished performance, with or without the Perfect Love!

In these days of social isolation, it's important to divide up the day with rituals and recently Bill has taken to appearing in my study in the late afternoon and announcing, in portentous tones, "cocktails will be served in the sitting room at six o'clock, Madam". I do like that "Madam". That's my cue to down my hot computer mouse, dive into a fresh frock, grab pearls, big earrings and lipstick, and settle down among the sofa cushions, ready to lie back and think of Mexico, margarita in hand. Because such an announcement has come to mean a margarita—just the one, mind—nothing mundane like a glass of wine.

Bill is making like M. Peychaud and putting meticulous care into his margarita production. I'm not surprised. He makes the best gin-and-tonic I've had anywhere: we think the clue is lime not lemon, not just a slice, but a decent squeeze. The exact extent of the squeeze, as in other forms of foreplay, is a closely guarded secret. Back to margaritas, the current recipe comes from a young Mexican friend of ours, Karla, whom we call The Tequila Slammer. Karla can sit for hours nursing a large tequila; equally, she can demolish it in seconds. Either way it seems to have no effect on her at all. So now I see Bill carefully measuring tequila, cointreau and lime juice in a tiny measuring glass, a bit like M. Peychaud's egg cup or *coquetier*. (Hence, the name 'cocktail'.) Each time he has been tinkering with the balance, varying the ingredients by the millilitre in search of the *équilibre parfait*. AND he dug out a couple of old cocktail glasses. Neither of us remembers why we have them or where they came from but, after years of lingering sorrowfully in some dark cupboard, they have emerged into the sunlight of usefulness and we are enjoying our rediscovery of this lovely drink. Bill bought a large quantity of limes this morning so I think a margarita may be in my future today!

Our current interest in margaritas was triggered by the emergence from a bookshelf, during our ongoing hunt for books to give away, of a rather delightful small volume called *Everyday Drinking. The Distilled Kingsley Amis* published by Bloomsbury in 2008. Christopher Hitchens, who wrote the Introduction to the book, claims that booze was Amis's muse and that he early grasped "the plain fact that [alcohol] makes other people, and indeed life itself, a good deal less boring". He claims further:

> . . . the famous hangover scene in *Lucky Jim*, not equalled for alcoholic comedy in our literature even by Shakespeare's night porter or portly knight, has only one rival . . . and that is Peter Fallow's appalling waking moment in Tom Wolfe's *The Bonfire of the Vanities*.

There's some re-reading for us all, or at least for me.

Sir Kingsley Amis described the margarita as "one of the most delicious drinks in the world" and he gives two versions in *Everyday Drinking*. One is rather messy and not to be recommended at all, particularly in these coronavirus times. He advises never to drink tequila on its own, noting that "even your humble peon will insist on his lime and salt". I can't see the following unsophisticated method translating into a Manhattan salon or, indeed, any other civilised place:

> Pour some table salt onto the back of your left hand round
> about the base of the thumb. Grip a slice of lime in your right
> hand. Have a tot of neat tequila standing by. As fast as possible,
> lick the salt, suck the lime, shut your eyes and drink up. (Some
> people do lime then salt).

Really? Perhaps among his 'humble peons'. I'm reminded of Mexico
and the *pulquerias* in backblocks villages which, in our day, used
to display a sign over the entrance saying "women and soldiers not
allowed". It seems that when *pulque* (a traditional central Mexican
alcoholic drink made from the fermented sap of the maguey, or
agave, plant) flowed things could get a bit willing and guns could be
drawn. Under such circumstances, pulque or tequila, any old method
might suffice!

I figure the rest of us would go for what Amis calls "a kind of dude's
version" of the above. The salt-rimmed glass, the tequila, lime juice
and cointreau mixture (shaken or stirred!) with ice. Amis's recipe is
three parts tequila, two parts fresh lime juice and one part Cointreau
but, he warns, "*por Dios, Señor,* watch it! After three of the same I
once had the most violent quarrels I have ever had with a female, and
in Mexico City too—but luckily we were both unarmed at the time".
Remember that sign! Bill doesn't use Kingsley Amis's proportions. We
prefer to heed Amis's warning and follow Karla's far gentler recipe!

This is the seventh week I've been writing to you all and I've
very much enjoyed the sense of connection it has given me. I hope
it has done the same for you. Thank you for your many responses
and, particularly during this last week, for sharing your stories about
ANZAC Day or experiences of similar remembrance. I shall continue
writing and look forward to hearing from you. Who knows how
long the present circumstances of community lockdown and social
distancing will continue but what will definitely continue is friendship
and that is worth nurturing.

So, this evening I will happily settle down to one modest margarita,
thinking of places we've lived and how every culture seems to have
developed the arts of brewing and fermenting. Hitchens says such
arts open everyone to "regions infernal as well as paradisiac" and
I think he's right. How interesting to wonder, he remarks, how the
Italian word for bottle, *fiasco,* has come to be used as it is in English.

I will raise my glass to you all. *Salut! Mahbruk! Selamat Kesehatan! Your very good health!*

Keep safe and keep well

With love

Elaine
4 May 2020

PS. Bill is keeping very quiet about having facilitated the introduction of Corona from Mexico to Australia in 1988 but I am blowing his cover.

PPS. Corona the beer, not the virus!

8
The Contented Sole

Dear Friends,

New shoes, new shoes,
Red and pink and blue shoes.
Tell me, what would you choose,
If they'd let us buy?
Buckle shoes, bow shoes,
Pretty pointy-toe shoes,
Strappy, cappy low shoes;
Let's have some to try.
Bright shoes, white shoes,
Dandy-dance-by-night shoes,
Perhaps-a-little-tight shoes,
Like some? So would I.
BUT
Flat shoes, fat shoes,
Stump-along-like-that shoes,
Wipe-them-on-the-mat shoes,
That's the sort they'll buy.

I'm wearing playing-ladies shoes today. That means not lace-ups, not
"stump-along-like-that shoes" which is what I've had to wear since
having polio as a child. When I'm being sensible, that is, which I'm
not all the time. Frida Wolfe's little poem *Choosing Shoes* has a nice
defiant tone that resonates with me! Until I was about twelve the
only shoes I had were flat, black and laced up. Mind you, they were
accessorised—with calipers! I occasionally wonder how I could have
ended up working in a field where black shoes are the uniform. Your
average priest, male or female, tends not to go in for wild colours with
sequin trims—not, at least, when they're on the job. Actually, I don't
go in for sequin trims myself.

So playing-ladies shoes for me are flat but with NO laces and, when I'm lucky, with bows. I'm not sure I thought about it much until teenage years struck along with all that angst, flame-faced self-consciousness and who-am-I stuff. Then the other girls were getting their first high heels and I longed for anything but "wipe-them-on-the-mat shoes". I remember one awful occasion before a school dance when the girls were admiring their new dresses and new shoes (with heels) and their eyes fell to mine and a Great Silence fell upon us. That's a teenage moment of wanting to die.

It was probably also a bit of a wake-up moment when I first realised that, if I could wear high heels, I'd opt for the highest most outrageous stilettos I could find. None of that Theresa May kitten heel nonsense. I'd swan around in Louboutin and the like, ruining my bank balance and my Achilles tendons, and spending more time than anyone ought in physiotherapists' rooms getting sorted out. Despite high heels being dream territory—maybe because—I am inordinately interested in shoes. I notice what other people are wearing—and whether they are clean and polished. When our friend John retired from the Australian foreign service one testimonial noted that he had worn "the most polished shoes in the diplomatic service". Everyone laughed but I thought that, regardless of all John's achievements, that was an accolade of which to be proud! He was such an improvement in every way on our first ambassador, who had really small feet and wore quite nasty plaited shoes. See what I mean? I notice.

As it happens, I have a pair of plaited shoes. They are tan and highly polished and Italian and I paid more for them than any shoes I've ever bought. I love them but woe! In the late nineties, I had an operation on my left foot to try to stabilise it a bit. The next morning my surgeon said, "Oh, by the way, I took the opportunity to relax the tendons so that foot will be a bit longer now". My first thought was, "Oh my God, what about my Italian shoes! Thanks, Max!" I still have those shoes. They are the ultimate in playing-ladies-shoes but I can't walk in them at all. Still, I take them out now and again, squeeze them on and sit. And think how pretty they are. And I have forgiven Max.

I also have a pair of shoes with huge bows, the biggest I've seen on any shoes. They're blue suede, with blue chiffon bows which flop this way and that very satisfyingly. They are very much 'you-think-you've-got-bows!' shoes and bad for one's personal pride. Just for fun, I wore them to church once when I was preaching and referred to them, and that I was wearing them, to illustrate some point or other. Later in the service, at the moment when people greet each other, a voice called out, "Show us your bows!" I swanned down the aisle holding up my robes as people crowded forward to see Elaine's bows. There was a noticeable and happy sense of community in the church that day. The Rector, who wasn't there, would have disapproved, not of the atmosphere, but of me.

Community and shoes took a different turn one awful day thirteen years ago when we were in Jakarta. A Garuda plane crashed at Jogjakarta airport killing twenty one people, including four Australian Embassy officers and an Australian journalist. The Embassy community was deeply upset, as it had been when the Embassy was bombed in 2004, and would be twice more during our time by terrorist-related deaths. One young woman was particularly affected. She'd been at the scene of the crash and her shoes—red, as it happens—were ruined in the mud of the rice fields as she tried to get to the site and her colleagues. Some days later, Bill's wonderful deputy, Louise, stated emphatically, "What a girl needs at moments like this are shopping and shoes!" And off they went. Marvellous new red stilettos were the cure. I sighed deeply with longing when I saw them!

Recently I found an extraordinary suggestion about shoes in a book called *Take a Spare Truss. Tips for Nineteenth Century Travellers.* It's an amusing compilation of suggestions for British travellers and includes some gob-smacking insights into a society in which, as it says on the flyleaf, "the British had no doubt that Britain was Top Nation". It quotes one Mrs C. E. Humphries in 1897 on the British traveller's duty: "It ought to be part of our patriotic feeling to endeavour to convey as agreeable an idea as possible of ourselves to those countries which we honour with our distinguished presence in our little trips". Breathtaking! The tip that took my eye concerns blisters on the feet:

> It not infrequently happens that the feet of those not thoroughly accustomed to hard tramping will become blistered. When the eggs of either poultry or wild birds are to be obtained, it is a good plan to break one or two, according to their size, into each shoe before starting in the morning.

I don't think so. It definitely wouldn't work with strappy sandals. And, by the way, there is also the suggestion that rubbing feet morning and evening with brandy and tallow will prevent blistering. I don't think I'll bother with that either and I don't drink brandy but I'd have thought that, in the evening after a long day's tramping, one's thoughts might settle on drinking the stuff rather than rubbing it on one's feet.

Speaking of drinking, thank you for your responses and suggestions about cocktails. I'm ignoring my friend Dean who thinks he might write a book called *The Plastered Priest*! Lyn wrote of savouring rum sours while watching the sun set in Bagan in Myanmar and I have to say that one of my magic moments was sailing gently on the Irrawaddy from Bagan to Mandalay, a beautifully cold gin-and-tonic to hand, reading George Orwell's *A Clergyman's Daughter*. It was so apt. And to those who want to compare cocktail-making skills with Bill's, all I can say is, when we are allowed to travel again, we look forward to your attempts!

Tonight before cocktail hour I think I will put on my purple suede playing-ladies shoes (yes, purple, Elvis, how could you get that so wrong?), a rich dark purple. Or I might wear the red suede with black flowers. Either way I'll make like I'm catwalking at a fashion show. That'll be a failure, of course, but a little imagination and one margarita are quite enough to be getting on with. Oh, and I've been browsing the Louboutin website and have discovered they sell FLAT SHOES. I must check my bank balance.

In honour of shoes, there is a wonderful painting of the Last Supper by Australian artist Graeme Drendel hanging in the chapel of St Andrew's College, Sydney University. I love its originality AND its seven pairs of women's shoes under the table—which allows for the idea that women (like Mary Magdalene and others) were among the disciples of Jesus. This painting gives me the chance to tell a favourite Maundy Thursday joke which I really can't use when preaching on that day. Think of any Last Supper painting you've ever seen. Jesus and disciples gathered to share a meal and all on one side of the table. Anyone who has ever tried to maintain good dinner table conversation seated like that knows it's definitely not the way to seat people! Be that as it may, Jesus is saying, "OK, guys, anyone who wants to be in the picture, get on this side of the table!"

Have a good week. Keep well and keep safe

With love

Elaine
11 May 2020

9
Miss Bonny Bunny Comes Home

Dear Friends,

Social distancing rules have been eased slightly in Canberra so we have been able to entertain friends again. Yesterday was particularly special. There were six of us at lunch: Bill's former Deputy in Jakarta, three former Australian Ambassadors, our current 'man in Jakarta'— and me, who would once have been thought of as a trailing spouse. To observe distancing requirements, we needed to move the dining room table to another room so, as Bill's successor as Ambassador— now the Australian Secretary for Defence—lives around the corner, he and his muscles were called upon during the morning to help Bill. Thanks Greg. If ever there was an occasion for creaking over old times yesterday was it. Lots of fun. Thank you, friends. 'Back to Jakarta' will reconvene soon.

I had some good news this week which is a really nice thing to happen in these difficult times. However, it's a little complicated so let me tell you a story . . .

Ten years ago, while we were still in Jakarta, I flew down to Australia to help our daughter, Catherine, when she was about to have her third child. A couple of days before Clio (named for daughter of Zeus and muse of history!) was born I took care of the older girls, Tess and Mimi, one afternoon while their mother rested. There was much activity as they prepared a game with all their dolls and toys— setting up a little theatre. As you may know, small children can spend half an hour setting up a game and it's over in two minutes. I had noticed that one toy was a large white rabbit with a missing eye and, needing to spin out the time for their mother's sake, I made up a story for them about this rabbit.

Fast forward some weeks and back in Jakarta, I took myself off one morning armed with a yellow legal pad (I didn't have a laptop then) and ensconced myself in the atrium lounge of the Hyatt Hotel at Plaza Indonesia. There, plied with several rounds of coffee over an hour or two, I wrote the story of Tess and Mimi's rabbit: *Miss Bonny Bunny Loses An Eye*. I'd never written a children's story before and I'm not quite sure what prompted me to write it down that day. Whatever the reason, Miss Bonny Bunny was born. Numbers of friends got rather enthusiastic about it. Our friend Peter had people in his business set it out in proper publishing style. Another friend, Melba, the then Mexican Ambassador in Indonesia, wrote to a friend in Mexico City, Laura Marin, a children's book illustrator, who said, "Me gustan mucho las aventuras de Miss Bonny Bunny" (I love the adventures of Miss Bonny Bunny) and produced the most enchanting paintings of Miss Bonny Bunny and her friends Ginny Giraffe, Tilly Tortoise, Hetty Horse, Kitty Kangaroo and Leonora Lion. Interestingly, without any prompting at all, nobody, but nobody, ever refers to 'the rabbit'. As if they'd dare! She has always been Miss Bonny Bunny.

The book was published privately in Jakarta and it was great fun to give copies to people with children or grandchildren and even more fun to get reports from all over of how well it was received. Our friend and former Foreign Minister Gareth Evans read the book and, those of you who know Gareth will not be surprised to hear, offered a range of suggestions for improvement. Miss Bonny Bunny herself later wrote to Gareth when he was awarded Australia's highest honour (not, incidentally, for services to children's literature)!

Amid all the fuss as we left Indonesia, we forgot that cartons of copies of the book were stored in Peter's warehouse. Some years later he, too, left Indonesia and now has written saying the books are in his Melbourne warehouse and waiting to be delivered as soon as coronavirus travel restrictions allow him to bring them. So Miss Bonny Bunny is coming home. I am delighted.

I should add here another Jakarta story of the time when our then-pregnant daughter-in-law, Jessica, pulled a rabbit from the hat in rather spectacular style. Then Prime Minister John Howard was making a state visit to Indonesia and, on the morning of the state lunch, news came that Jessica had gone into labour. While President Yudhoyono and our Prime Minister held talks, attended by Bill and others, Ibu Ani Yudhoyono, Mrs Howard, various ladies and I were together and excitement ran high about the birth that was taking place. There are ways and ways of cementing international relations and we women did our bit that morning, bonding as we swapped birth stories and the Indonesian ladies sent messages to Jessica saying "push!" News of the baby's arrival came in the middle of the state lunch. Jemima Cecily had been born. I burst into tears. Everyone leapt to their feet; the President and the Prime Minister pumped each other's hands and beamed as if they were the proud grandfathers; Ibu Ani and I and all the ladies cried and hugged. The security men—both Indonesian and Australian—were utterly bemused, edging forward with hands to weapons! It was certainly an original state occasion. We have kept the official menu card signed by the President and the Prime Minister. Mr Howard wrote, "To Jemima, welcome to the world". Quite a keepsake.

Miss Bonny Bunny is not the only publishing adventure I had while in Indonesia. There was also . . . *And the Angels Held Their Breath,* a book of sermons subtitled *Sixteen Reasons for Exploring the God-Option* published in 2008 by the Australasian Theological Forum. Such a long time ago. I found myself reflecting recently that I don't preach like that any more. Fortunately. Any preacher worth his or her salt needs to change and develop—which is why publishing books of sermons is problematical. I still have some copies but I think I'll be able to move Miss Bonny Bunny more easily.

Be that as it may be, that little collection of sermons was eventually, through no effort on my part, translated into Bahasa Indonesia and published by the Jesuits in Indonesia! . . . *Dan Para Malaikat Pun Menahan Napas* was launched privately at our residence in Jakarta by an eminent Jesuit, Prof. Dr Father ("Romo") Franz-Magnis Suseno, SJ. Franz-Magnis is a German aristocrat who, after ordination, left Germany and his noble title for Jakarta where he teaches philosophy as well as working with the poor and in interfaith relations. A lovely man; I was honoured both by his friendship and having him launch my slim volume. What was so amusing, and oiled the wheels of a very happy launch party, was his pointing out that my book had been granted both a *Nihil Obstat* and an *Imprimatur* by the Catholic authorities in Indonesia. Franz-Magnis merrily noted that that meant I, a woman and a priest, had been declared to be free of all heresy. I am a little bit proud of that!

Back to Miss Bonny Bunny, I have written twice more of her adventures. The other tales are *Miss Bonny Bunny Bakes a Cake* and *Miss Bonny Bunny Buys a New Hat.* It is rather strange that I have written stories about a rabbit given that I grew up on the land in Australia and a mantra of those long ago days was "the only good rabbit is a dead rabbit". In rural Australia then there were rabbit inspectors whose job it was to check properties to ensure owners were doing all in their power to control the rabbit plague, killing all rabbits they found and digging out all rabbit burrows. My father was assiduous in this duty, so much so that, even though he killed many rabbits—actually, I think, because of that—he would never have rabbit cooked in our house. An easy, cheap source of protein one might have thought but it was banned during my childhood. I did not eat rabbit until I lived in England many years later.

But Miss Bonny Bunny was different. She was no plague rabbit. She was white and fluffy and imaginary. Nor was Emily, another rabbit about whom I have written a story, a plague rabbit. Emily belonged to our friend Christine in Boston. Emily was allegedly a French miniature lop-eared rabbit and when she was acquired she was extremely cute and all those things except none of us spoke rabbit— or should that be *lapin*—so we couldn't check the French connection. Very quickly, however, her credentials became very suss. Her ears sprang northward, then she began to grow apace. And she grew and grew, not only in size, but in boldness as well. So bold was Emily that she challenged Sam, the household's large German Shepherd. Emily was partial to dog food! Understandably, Sam was protective of his rights and food and we sometimes wondered what mayhem would result when Emily got too close. He didn't mind her cleaning up his scraps but no way was she sharing access to his food.

Emily's problem was that her appetite was prodigious. Not only was she partial to dog food, she trimmed every house plant she could reach. It reminded me of the way sheep on the farm trimmed the willow trees so neatly and evenly in straight horizontal lines! Eventually Christine bought a baby gate for the bottom of the stairs so Emily was confined to the plants on the ground floor. However, I'm afraid there was more and this is where writing a children's story about Emily became challenging. Emily was prone to chewing electrical wires and, you've guessed it, eventually she was electrocuted. I haven't worked out how to finish Emily's story. I'm not sure that modern children would handle a story ending "and then she died—zapped and frizzled". Perhaps I could get away with it if I leave out those last three words? I am reminded of Struwwelpeter and fingers being cut off. Were we all just tougher because we survived such children's tales?

Miss Bonny Bunny and Emily. I've been asked why I don't do something to try to have them published. The obvious first answer is that I'd hate to have them knocked back. And they might well be. They're just fantasy—except for Emily. They don't push any political agenda. I'm not trying to educate children in any way of thinking. They're just meant to be fun. Miss Bonny Bunny and her friends are all female but that's because the names matched. And then there are the lovely illustrations. They'd be ditched because Australian publishers would want to create their own and I can't see my imaginary toys in a different form. So I've let it be. Fear of rejection is always strong, isn't it?

Which is no excuse, of course. I probably need someone to nag me. I've suggested to Bill that he be chief nagger but he says, "that's not *my* job". By the look on his face I think he's making a point but what could that possibly be? If anyone wants the position of 'chief nagger' do let me know!

In the meantime, Miss Bonny Bunny will soon be home. I will make her a special supper. She's rather partial to the sharp peppery flavour of arugula so I will add lots to the mignonette she also fancies. She doesn't drink but I might be able to persuade her to a thimble of dandelion wine—for her health's sake—and to toast all my other friends wherever you are.

By the way, Bill pleads no more bunny stories. He says it could be rabbit-forming and we've got enough Bugs around at the moment. Oh dear.

Go well and keep safe.

With love

Elaine
18 May 2020

10
Tales of Grace for a Plague Year

Dear Friends,

I mentioned last week that here in Canberra we are now allowed to entertain small numbers of people provided we observe social distancing regulations. So we have two tables set up in T-form, meaning we can be six in all without breaking any rules. We're both enjoying a return to hospitality, which has got me thinking. Hospitality seems sidelined at the moment, the word itself used only in relation to an industry. I read an article recently about missing friends and the word 'hospitality' didn't even feature. The focus *du jour* seems very much on individuals rather than community. This is understandable but says little beyond how *we* feel, which is not the whole point. Hospitality's about giving, not just receiving. It's about the other person, not just giving a cup of tea or coffee, a meal, or a glass of wine.

Hospitality's not about changing someone. It means creating a space where someone can feel safe and welcomed. In extreme terms, that means where enemy can become friend. It's about not fearing them or the differences they may present. So this week I want to tell you about three times in my life that demonstrated that kind of openness, from my two worlds, the diplomatic, the church, and from where the two met.

Cairo, and our first posting. I was very young, very green and very ignorant. Being in Egypt was a huge adventure and diplomatic life, about which I knew nothing apart perhaps from odd references in a book or two, was a challenge. And I took some body blows. Don't we all on the road to becoming grown-ups. (Am I one yet? That's not for today . . .) I won't go into details—it was so long ago—but I fell foul of the ambassador (the one with the little feet in plaited

43

shoes I mentioned a couple of weeks back). In effect, power met powerlessness and I was flattened.

The ambassador summoned his secretary one day and dictated a letter to the foreign ministry in Canberra requesting Bill's recall. The letter was never sent. Susie, his secretary, refused to type it. There was a row which apparently involved a broken typewriter, but she won the day. Then Susie took me away for a few days saying, "I'm going to teach you what diplomatic life is all about". Her most startling comment was "you're not to blame for this attack. I know that you are scared silly about this life. I know you walk into a room terrified about making a mistake or not being able to think of a thing to say. But the reality is that when you walk into a room your head is high, your gaze is firm and you look in total control. You look the part even if you don't feel it; the boss can't stand that."

I'm ashamed to say I tried some personal re-education after that. I'd lock myself in the bedroom and practise holding my head down and peeping out from the side. The meek and demure look. Proper, quiet, controlled and obedient. Dear God. It didn't last long because I got bored and simply forgot to apply my 'lessons'. Years later I was reminded of those lonely lessons when I saw footage of the young Diana, Princess of Wales. She seemed to do naturally what I tried to teach myself to do. Both of us grew up and held our heads as high as we wanted. Though I never got to do a photoshoot at the Taj Mahal. Damn. And the real end of this story? Susie had opened a door, taught me a few tricks, and said, in essence, "being you is just fine". Hospitality is about honouring each individual, and allowing them in—to our lives, to our worlds.

Many years later, older, wiser and cannier, we were in Papua New Guinea where I encountered the Papal Nuncio, an elegant Spanish archbishop. After we first met he went out of his way to avoid doing so again. He was challenged by a Catholic friend who pointed out that it wasn't acceptable not to speak to me just because I was a woman and a priest. The Catholic Church, he ploughed on stoutly, doesn't accept the ordination of women but it does countenance courtesy. The barb found its mark. During an American 4th of July reception the Nuncio suddenly appeared at my elbow and proceeded to engage me in a lengthy conversation—about liturgy! Talking shop!

Some time later Bill and I attended an ordination for new Catholic priests, and the Nuncio was leading the ceremonies. At the point when people greet each other with a handshake as a sign of God's peace, the Nuncio shook hands only with the Catholic priests then strode down the aisle, a very long aisle, past everyone else—to me. He exchanged the peace with me, a female priest. (By the way, not with the senior diplomat there—Bill!) It was a deeply moving gesture of acceptance—the heart of hospitality—not lost on observers in that vast cathedral, and I struggled to maintain composure. The rest of our acquaintance was friendly and open. When we said goodbye at the end of his posting we shook hands, perhaps holding a little longer than would be usual. We smiled at each other in that way you do when you have shared a particular experience and he left my life, a man who had struggled with a formal stricture of his church but allowed the obligation to hospitality within the Christian gospel to win. We may not belong to the same church, the Nuncio's gesture said, but we do not close doors upon each other. We are to treat together, in mutual acceptance, whether as nations or churches—just as we are. That is grace.

My third and final story about hospitality takes us to Malaysia and the Anglican cathedral, St Mary's, in Kuala Lumpur. The church there—conservative Evangelical Anglican—didn't recognise me as priest so my presence was, I guess, confronting. Yet I was allowed to preach and the first time was, for me at least, unforgettable.

I had no way of predicting responses but I arrived during the early service so I could robe alone before anyone could tell me not to. Trading on diplomatic experience and the people's innate politeness, I suspected I would not be challenged if found already robed. And I wasn't. The Dean, Jason Selvaraj, now Suffragan Bishop of West Malaysia, is an intelligent and thoughtful man, and his response to what happened was courageous and humbling. With grace and dignity, he invited me to join the procession and conducted me to an archdeacon's stall. I preached from the pulpit. All firsts for a woman in that place. Only once had a woman preached in that cathedral before. Not robed, she had sat in the congregation with her husband, then preached from the chancel step below the pulpit.

It was a complex situation. I had lived too long in the diplomatic world to be unaware that customs are to be respected, not flouted. I was a guest with the concomitant obligation to respect different ways. But I was also a priest, under obligation to behave as such. I had to demonstrate equality with the men, and not shrink from challenge and rejection. Finally, I had become an icon for many Anglican women in Kuala Lumpur who wanted women ordained and would be watching keenly to see how I behaved and what would happen. It is not comfortable to be anyone's icon.

The gospel lesson that day could not have been more pointedly appropriate. Jesus's parable of the man who invites people to dinner but his potential guests cry off. Servants are sent to invite others including "the poor, the crippled, the blind, and the lame"; in other words, outsiders, strangers. The situation that day begged the question: who is the stranger to God? In my sermon, I made no political statements about groups the Church in various places had effectively rendered 'strangers', such as homosexuals and women. (That's not totally changed.) There was no need and it would have been impolite—a violation of hospitality. The message was given by my presence, robed, processing, preaching from the pulpit—if anyone wanted to hear it.

Jason heard. On his face I saw a great battle being fought out: gospel against institution and doctrine; faith against culture; change against tradition. Gospel, faith, and openness to change won. He invited me to the altar for the Great Thanksgiving. After the Words of Institution he stepped back and gestured to me to complete the prayer. He administered communion to me and then held out his hands to receive the bread and wine from me. He invited me to administer the bread to the people. None of this had ever happened there before and it happened then because God whispered to one man's heart that he might be hearing God's truth, and not just the voice of the world and its ways. And he responded, courageously and graciously. There was a price for him. Numbers of priests present that morning walked out. When told later what had happened, his bishop held his peace but not all his fellow priests did. Jason was too discreet to tell me but others did.

The last time I preached at St Mary's Cathedral, as I stepped into the pulpit, Jason came forward and announced to the congregation that he had changed his position and now believed that unless the Church ordained women to the priesthood, it was representing a fractured body of Christ. It was hard to continue, knowing myself the recipient of the grace of true hospitality: a gift to the stranger of space to be who she was rather than what some preferred that she be.

It's been quite sobering revisiting memories of these occasions when I have been accorded such hospitality. Susie, the Papal Nuncio in PNG, and Jason Selvaraj in Malaysia; none of them needed to have done what they did. Susie could have left a lonely and insecure girl to fend for herself but instead opened a door to acceptance and possibility. Jason could have stood firmly on the ground of his form of Anglicanism's trenchant rejection of ordaining women. The Nuncio could have stood on the same ground, saying "we are the one true church and all else is to be rejected". Three actions where the hand of hospitality was extended and someone's life—mine—was made that much happier.

There is a story about a priest who spent his life serving pilgrims at a hostel for pilgrims on the Camino, that long walk from France through Spain to St James's shrine in Santiago de Compostela. In 2002, a British TV crew, a self-proclaimed faithless and irreverent lot, went to record his story and that of the others who worked as servants for the pilgrims. They understood the idea of pilgrimage but not what those who served them were about. "What have you all been doing?" they asked. "Oh," said the old priest, "just changing the world, that's all . . ."

Quite. Each story is one step towards a better world. Especially when times are challenging. A little while ago when loo paper hoarding seemed the main reaction to the pandemic here, a friend asked a supermarket cashier whether there was any available and the woman replied, "No, but I took these for myself so you have them". Retrieving a packet from under the counter, she pressed them upon our friend. A small gesture, which was a big gesture, and full of grace.

And now, a final story that has given me joy this week. I told you last week about Miss Bonny Bunny and now it seems I am to be pursued by the fluffy things. The following story isn't mine but I have been given permission to tell it.

It's about an 11-year old girl called Emily and her pet. Emily had long wanted a rabbit and her parents finally obliged. Enter young Pearl. Some months later, on instruction from the vet, Emily and her father took Pearl for de-sexing. After examining Pearl, the vet sat Emily down for a serious talk, ignoring Emily's father completely. "Emily, I'm sorry, I was wrong," the vet said. "Pearl has a bifurcated penis—do you know what a penis is?" Emily nodded seriously. The word 'bifurcated' was then explained—more serious nodding.

"Well this means that when he was born his penis was so very tiny it looked like a vagina—do you know what that is?" Yes, and the serious nodding continued as Emily took it all in and her father bit his cheeks and wished he had a fork to stick in his thigh to prevent his laughing. "So we thought she was a girl, but she is more a he." The vet concluded, "So Pearl is actually transgender and now I will have to ask you to come back in a few months for him to be snipped—he is too small yet for that surgery." Emily has renamed her bunny with the elegant handle of Harry/Pearl.

So now we have transgender bunnies! And I was concerned about ending my story about Emily the French allegedly miniature lop-eared bunny's being electrocuted, zapped and frizzled! Children can handle much more than many people think. By the way, can anyone tell me why female rabbits can be desexed earlier than males? Same with kittens—I went through that with Sam and Anxious, Julian and Catherine's kittens in New York.

But that, my friends, is a story for another day.

Keep well and keep safe,

With love
Elaine
25 May 2020

11
Sad, Sad, Sad

Dear Friends,

I have felt flattened this week. Not by the pandemic's restrictions, though watching the continually rising statistics of deaths is depressing enough. Flattened more by the terrible news out of the States. Cities in flames. Rioting and rage. Understandable rage. Impossible to fathom how a police officer could think it allowable to kneel on someone's neck and then refuse to heed distress and warnings till death ended the sordid affair. Not allowable under any circumstances, surely, but *murder*. And for what? But there has been more. An Afro-American birdwatcher in New York arrested on the basis of a dodgy call to police. Arrested because he was black and the caller was a white woman. She was disobeying park regulations requiring dogs to be on leads. The accused pointed this out. Did she trade on the unspoken power wielded by some women calling foul on a black man because they know they'll be believed? At least that's the suggestion by one writer in the *New York Times* and it's not hard to think it credible. She's apologised, and lost her job, but she should never have done it.

I've thought often during the week of *The Bonfire of the Vanities*, Tom Wolfe's book from 1997, about the young New York investment banker, Sherman McCoy, whose life was a mess. Walking his reluctant and bad-tempered dog one wet night:

> . . . Sherman was aware of a figure approaching him. It was . . .
> a black youth, tall, rangy, wearing white sneakers. Sherman
> stared at him. Well, let him come! I'm not budging! . . . I'm
> not giving way for any street punks! The black youth suddenly
> made a ninety-degree turn and cut straight across the street to

the sidewalk on the other side. The feeble yellow of a sodium-vapor streetlight reflected for an instant on his face as he checked Sherman out. He had crossed over! What a stroke of luck! Not once did it dawn on Sherman McCoy that what the boy had seen was a thirty-eight-year-old white man, soaking wet, dressed in some sort of military-looking raincoat full of straps and buckles, holding a violently lurching animal in his arms, staring, bug-eyed, and talking to himself.

The point is sharp and clear and funny but the lesson here isn't really funny at all. Especially when we think that it's mostly still the Sherman McCoys who get to be the insiders and the black guys—rangy, young or otherwise—who don't.

My American friends will also have been devastated by all this and let me hasten to add that we in Australia don't have a good record in race relations either. Much treatment of indigenous Australians in the 232 years since European settlement has been awful. Massacres, violence and abuse. Not counted as people in the census till 1971 after a 1967 referendum decreed that they should be included. It's said in Australia that it's so difficult to get referenda passed that you could have a referendum for free beer and it'd fail. But in this case it passed because the Australian people knew it was the right thing to do. That does not mean that racial discrimination and abuse are dead. They aren't. There has been lifelong damage and trauma to the Stolen Generation, those indigenous babies and children taken from their families to be brought up in white families. Often trained only to be servants in white homes—as in my maternal grandparents' home. Aboriginal deaths in police custody are a national scandal. Aboriginal numbers in prisons are a serious concern. Social problems in aboriginal areas are rife and health and education indicators show continuing indigenous disadvantage.

Today is Reconciliation Day in Australia and I have been sitting listening to music by contemporary indigenous Australian composers. There is sadness in their music, but hope too, reflections of their lived reality in contemporary Australia. Today we acknowledge that we have come some way to national reconciliation in recent decades but have a long way to go. On a personal note, our household is well aware of this, Bill having been Secretary for five years of federal departments dealing with indigenous affairs; and my nephew, Jeremy, is a legal advocate in Sydney dealing with indigenous clients.

Racism seems to be an insidious evil lodged deep in the human gut. And it isn't just white against non-white. I've seen forms in every country I've lived in, from people of all races. That's not an excuse, just an observed fact of my experience. I wish it were not so but somehow some people seem incapable of resisting the easy self-protection of attacking that which is different and makes them afraid or wary. And, when they have the power to attack, they just do.

For myself, all I can say is that I am relieved I said to Bill decades ago, when Julian and Catherine were babies, that I'd go anywhere with him and his job except South Africa. I feared the insidious effect of Apartheid on our children. Bill didn't need persuading. And I'm proud of the stand Julian took when visiting us in Papua New Guinea. He went to a club with Papua New Guinean friends and was standing with them in shadow inside the entrance when a man—a white man—called out, "Hey, boy, open the door!" Julian 'spoke Australian' to him, as we say, which means he told him where to get off. The man left. I admired Julian's courage in standing up for simple decency. Laughing it off with the man would have been easy but it would also have been joining him in his racism. Julian resisted the easy way, in the face of possible attack, and he was only twenty at the time. I am proud of him.

As I was proud, decades later, of our granddaughter Tess and her response to the first black person she had seen. Only four at the time, she went with her family to visit friends and to meet their overseas visitors. Barely through the door, Tess halted, rigid and staring, deaf to her parents' attempts to move her along. She stared at these strangers: the woman red-haired with pale Irish colouring; the man dark-skinned, from the Caribbean. She hadn't been taught colour prejudice; she simply hadn't seen a dark-skinned person in her short life. The child stared and stared; everybody was acutely conscious of the scene. They tried to talk but conversation became more and more stilted as tension and anxiety burdened the air around them. My daughter found herself silently begging God, "Don't let her do the wrong thing PLEASE!" Just when it seemed a happy afternoon was going to be smashed into unseemly pieces, Tess moved. She walked over to the man, touched his arm and said, "you have beautiful skin". A racist world, that sees the difference of black skin as a negative, shown up by a child who saw in the difference, beauty. My black American friend, Clayton, inured to a world of rejection, a strong and successful man for all that, cried when he heard this simple tale. He should never have had to shed tears over such rejection—he should never have had to endure it.

It was strangely congruent that during this sad and confronting week, in our ongoing attempt to divest ourselves of too many books, I reread an old book whose name takes me back to my childhood, *Letters of an Indian Judge to an English Gentlewoman.* It was one of my mother's favourite books and the last one she read in the hospice as she was dying. It's an elegant book, originally published in 1934, of purportedly-real letters written in the dying days of the British Raj in India and Burma. Whether it is fiction or non-fiction, or a blend, is an unresolvable issue; the author remains anonymous. The letters trace a 'literary friendship' which began with a single meeting between a young Indian just returned from Cambridge and an Englishwoman at a large Government House party in Calcutta. She engaged the lonely young man in conversation and he, grateful for her kindness, wrote to thank her.

The book traces not just their lives (all the letters are from him to her—Lady Sahib), but the difficulties and racism he encountered in his career. He is perceptive in his commentary on both the British imperial system in India and Burma and on British traditions and the caste system in Britain itself. His reflections on Indian customs and education, and feeling caught between his inherited traditions and the preferences education had instilled in him, are frequently sad and always poignant. He has an acute eye and an intelligent wit that spies racism and his observations to Lady Sahib are sharply accurate, even if gently told. He demonstrates both nobility and humility throughout his life as he balances moving through several worlds, including old and emerging India, and the best and the worst of British culture. I felt it would have been a privilege to know him.

This is one book that I will not be getting rid of. Do read it if you have a chance. It is charming, with a deep undercurrent of experience, sadness, wit, resilience and grit—the better side of humankind. I can't resist giving you just this one quotation. He writes to Lady Sahib of visiting the Burmese Golden Pagoda with its many statues of Buddha:

> Standing up there in the sunshine and the stillness, I think again of Westminster Abbey which I love very dearly. For there one finds the same stillness, the same stone statues, only

they are of gentlemen with beards and swords. All manner of men surround their Gods with mystery and with stone figures, each to their different taste. Somewhere, I suppose, there is one God. We all approach him in our several ways, and fashion him in our likeness. We build Him temples of our fond imaginings. Whilst all the time no doubt He remains somewhere without, and laughs kindly at our toys.

Enough of sadness. Now I want to tell you an uplifting story about an Australian musical group that has become widely popular in recent years. I'd never heard of them until this week and I think that, in these troubled times, it's no bad thing to be able to comfort ourselves with laughter. In the remote and tiny town of Mullimbimby in northern New South Wales there is a men's choir, a bunch of ordinary blokes who sing only Russian songs in Russian, the sad songs, the dirges, they say, to bring joy in a time of pandemic! None of them is Russian, or has connections with Russia, or speaks Russian. They call themselves "the Dustyesky Choir from Mullumgrad" and practise at the local Returned Soldiers' Hall where, they say, the beer is good and free-flowing. A lot of them have grown beards, or adopted braces and wear big boots and workmen's caps. They look as if they are having fun playing with stereotypes: Russians out of old movies, and Australian larrikins with beers in hand.

One of their number does a great Russian accent and, looking like a bearded Russian intellectual in his round-rimmed glasses, explains that they have renamed Mullimbimby Mullumgrad and, no, none of them is related to "that Dostoevsky boy". "He write story that make you cry, we sing song that make you laugh." So look up www.dustyesky. com and have a laugh with Australia's very own genuine/fake Russian choir. By the way 'esky' is the Australian term for a portable cold box for picnics. This choir, it seems, goes nowhere without its beer. They have become hugely popular in Russia and were to have been touring there at the moment but for coronavirus closing down travel.

Let me leave you by saying that I still believe in the basic goodness of human beings even though some of them can be right bastards at times. To that end, I need to tell you about a little boy, Braxton, about whom I read the other day. Braxton is three and lives with his family on the land—his father is a wheat and barley grower. The photo in the paper showed Braxton skipping along ahead of his father, a sunshine boy, a head of wild messed-up golden curls, bright shining blue eyes and an enormous smile. A glowing picture of health, hope and innocence, Braxton wants to be a grain grower like his dad, who noted that the child, though only three, knows every inch of the place. "The other day," said his father, "Braxton was watching one of my friends trying to fix an old Land Rover. It wouldn't start and Braxton said, 'have you tried the killer switch, Graham?' Graham did, and it worked." Braxton's father added, "he'll be running this place by the time he's five!"

I, who could not tell a killer switch from a live one, wish you a happy week. May it be more sunshiny and dotted with hope than the last one.

Keep well and keep safe.

With love,

Elaine
1 June 2020

12
Hope . . . More Than the Stuff of Dreams

Dear Friends,

> We are such stuff
> As dreams are made on, and our little life
> Is rounded with a sleep. Sir, I am vexed.
> Bear with my weakness. My old brain is troubled.

It was my birthday last Thursday. Another year wiped from the slate! I refuse to say "my old brain" but I will admit to my ageing brain. I will also agree with Shakespeare's inference about the basic goodness of humankind. So, as an antidote to my last letter when I felt flattened and sad, let me say this week that my ageing brain is not troubled.

But I *am* vexed because we were to have arrived in the US this coming Thursday for a happy time of catching up with friends in New York, Boston and Connecticut. As we can't leave Australia at the moment, my only comment is "poo". On the other hand, this will not last and I am full of hope for future times together.

Hope is the thing that has been wandering round in my brain this week. It's popped up happily despite the gloom and shock of events in America. And in Australia, where we have had our own example this week of appallingly bad treatment by a white police officer of a young black teenager. Friends have been sending their impressions. Rebecca wrote from Virginia that she feels hopeful because the demonstrations say so powerfully that people have had enough of injustice, discrimination and ineptitude. Anger is demanding change. Andrew writes from New York that Fifth Avenue may be closed to traffic and many businesses boarded up but the troubles have shifted the focus from the virus. Robin, a friend from Sydney, wrote, "the news out of the US has been disturbing but I have hope in my heart for my friends there, and for justice and a better way forward". Another friend, Stephen, in a conversation about hope, brought up Immanuel Kant's three questions: what can I know? what must I do? what may I hope for? As he pointed out, these questions are as apposite as they ever have been.

Anger is demanding change and we each have to find our own answers to those three questions. Hence, I write on, and Bill and I, now we are allowed, gather our friends, especially the singles, to try to foster community, friendship and hope even if only in our tiny way. And I suppose it is the tiny stuff. The personal and easy to manage, not the public and political. There have been protests all over Australia this week—anger is demanding change—in support of American protesters against the institutional and systemic racism they detect and experience in their country, and objecting to the same things here. There have been more protests this weekend; in the middle of a health pandemic that makes a pretty powerful statement, as we wrestle with the dilemma of demonstrating in a good cause versus social distancing imperatives. Opinions, of course, are sharply divided.

In interesting and happy juxtaposition to political tensions, there has been a Beethoven festival this weekend on ABC Classic FM radio (that's like the American PBS and the British BBC). For weeks listeners have sent in requests for their favourites in preparation for a countdown from 100 to the top favourite. One listener's comment was read out; he simply said, "How good is life!" How right he is! And the winner was (drum roll) the Choral Symphony and its Ode to Joy.

Last week I referred to that Tom Wolfe classic *The Bonfire of the Vanities*. Interestingly, it is another Tom Wolfe book that came to mind for me this week, with its final message of hope. *I Am Charlotte Simmons* is a dark story and I remember moments as I read it, seeing the main character move almost inexorably into a vortex of pain and hopelessness, of wanting to scream "don't do it!" It is a story of human angst, the need to belong, and the heartache of being young and vulnerable. Charlotte Simmons is a brilliant student from the Blue Ridge Mountains in North Carolina. An area so remote nobody had ever heard of it, we are told, and nobody ever went there except climbers for the challenge of its mountains and hunters for the challenge of its wildlife.

Charlotte leaves for university—Dupont. She's keen, full of dreams, determined to succeed. At Dupont she is assaulted by difference. Her clothes are wrong. Her accent is wrong. Her ambitions don't fit. Her morals don't fit. She doesn't fit in a hothouse atmosphere of privilege, money, sex and debasement. She is almost friendless. Charlotte is determined to resist the shocking depravity, determined to rise above it to the top of the heap, even as she longs to be part of the tribe. It is a sadly familiar tale.

Almost inevitably, she is undone; events reduce her to self-loathing and worthlessness. One harrowing sleepless night she reaches into her childhood Sunday School memories and prays, "Now I lay me down to sleep, I pray the Lord my soul to keep", but adds, "dear Lord, descend in flight and take a soulless one away this night". But she remained stricken and crashed completely.

Rescue began through the support of a friend. He picked her up. Cared for her. Served her needs. Loved her, but took no advantage, adding sacrifice for her sake to loving service. He wasn't perfect; he resented the lack of compensation in their relationship. But he served. Eventually, trying to force her out of her slump and into reality, he challenged her to be herself. "What you're doing is plain wrong! You're throwing away a great mind and a great opportunity! Who gave you the right to do such a thing! Who the hell do you think you are? You're Charlotte Simmons! Be Charlotte Simmons!"

Enter the Christ figure. Not a make-believe figure in a fairy tale. Our lives are not fairy tales and this is the figure we all need at times, the friend who, even without knowing it, is 'the Christ' for us. But the Servant-Christ doesn't always speak in soft tones; sometimes the tone is abrasive, confronting, challenging, touching lips with coals. In her turn, Charlotte acted as 'the Christ' for others and it is intriguing to watch some of the book's characters emerging out of negativity or debasement into acting out of their better selves, trying to be what they were created to be. This suggests answers to Kant's questions. What can I know? Myself. What must I do? The best I can for peace and justice for others. What may I hope for? The same for myself. Bringing a little joy to someone else. And a hope-filled future. "How good is life", the radio listener said. True, but it's our efforts that help it remain so.

There have been many little moments of laughter and sunshine during this pandemic lockdown and a lot of them come from simple human actions. I'm not going to blather on with a long list but I remembered one just now that made me laugh. With schools closed in lockdown, parents have had to take up home schooling. Our friend Ben set up a classroom for his two children and appeared before them in gown and mortarboard. I'm sure they laughed but I'm also sure they sat up just that bit straighter before their father-turned-teacher. And they'll have a great story and a joyful memory.

Now, a piece of pandemic silliness. Ben has lent me a book called *Ask the Past. Pertinent and Impertinent Advice from Yesteryear*. From one Alessio Piemontese, in his tome from 1563, *The Second Part of the Secretes of Maister Alexis of Piemont* (I bet that's on your bedside tables), we have the following recipe for dyeing one's hair green. In today's world where the fashion seems to be for a wild range of hair colours, this one may be a goer:

> To dye Heare into a Greene coloure. Take fresh Capers, and distill theym, and washe your heare with the water of them in the sunne, and they will become greene.

On that note, which caused quite a battle with my computer's almost irrepressible spellcheck function (we fight constantly), I will leave you with two other comments from the Beethoven festival, both about the Ode to Joy. "It makes my heart swell," said a child, "so it's big enough for everyone in the universe." An adult listener simply called Beethoven's masterpiece "bloody brilliant"! Amen, I say, to both.

And so I leave you for another week, my ageing brain untroubled but full of hope.

Keep safe. Keep well

With love

Elaine
8 June 2020

13
Hogwarts in Stanwell Park

Dear Friends,

Stanwell Park . . . otherwise known as Frog Hollow apparently! We visited our daughter Catherine and her family for a couple of days this week. The week before social lockdown she and her husband Garth sold one house and bought another in Stanwell Park, a coastal suburb south of Sydney. The timing was not what they would have chosen but the new house is in a large slab of rainforest with a beautiful sea view so plenty of compensation. The morning after they moved in Catherine texted us saying, "nobody told me the sea is so noisy"! One week after lockdown, the dishwasher packed up. New dishwasher bought. Then the hot water system failed. Friendly neighbour turned up to meet them and promptly sent for his electrician father who fixed a minor fault.

Meanwhile, because of pandemic regulations, Garth began working from home and had his salary reduced, Catherine lost all but one of her work contracts, and home schooling was decreed for all children. Hogwarts in Stanwell Park. Joy. The big girls, Tess and Mimi, retreated to their rooms and, being self-motivated and dedicated, got on with the job alone or via Zoom classes. Clio at ten needed a bit more management and it fell to Catherine to dredge up her education training. Clio had been at her new school—tiny, with about 150 students and a wonderful old-fashioned school bell which has somehow survived modernisation—for only a short time before lockdown, but mothers began contacting Catherine to fill her in on the community and keep Clio connected with her new friends. Great stuff to ease the burdens of teaching and trying to set up a new home.

While the humans sorted themselves out, the family's six hens went exploring and started laying all over the neighbours' properties; there are no fences in their new enclave. Neighbours began turning up repatriating eggs and Catherine and Garth discovered they'd bought into a very tight-knit community of neighbours who look out for each other. Friendship added to sea view as compensation for the drama of moving. Now that the hens have checked out their new surrounds, they've taken to laying at home; in the meantime they wander where they please and keep everyone's properties leech-free! This is rainforest after all. The hens are looking particularly sleek.

The sounds of the sea, and croaking frogs in creeks and waterlily ponds, are a comforting backdrop at the end of busy days. However, while wildlife at a distance is fine, up close and personal can be quite another matter. Catherine opened her stove's grill the other day and found a one and a half foot long baby python curled up inside. Much screaming, and the whole household raced to the kitchen thinking she'd scalded or otherwise injured herself, only to find her both screaming and grasping a frantically wriggling snake which was immediately returned to the wild—outside. My daughter the snake wrangler. I doubt I could have acted so coolly and I know I would have screamed. I'd have died if it were a spider. Catherine has since contacted the previous owner to ask whether he'd had a problem with incursions from the wild. Ah, he said, some: two sugar gliders, one possum and an owl. An owl? The Hogwarts thing is temporary, for heaven's sake! Hopefully, these animal adventures will not be repeated, though the next day Garth did discover the baby python trying to slither under the front door and back into the warmth.

Now we've had our period of joint birthday celebrations and I'm pooped. Dinner at Julian's where the meal was as good as ever—he and Jessica are excellent cooks; three dinners given at home, one lunch at friends, and the two days away, then a friend for lunch yesterday. All very enjoyable but I'm hoping for a quiet week. Dinner at home on Friday was great fun. Black tie and posh frocks as antidote to the grey weeks of isolation. Bill looking frightfully elegant, surrounded by an apparent harem of five women. Hummus soup with Greek yoghurt and dukkah, venison casserole (red currant jelly and a whole bottle of red wine in this one!), and Louise made a stunning blackberry and raspberry chocolate cake. And, by the way, I successfully made an Ottolenghi cake for one of these dinners: a thyme and honey cheesecake with white chocolate. No wonder everyone is complaining of weight gains during lockdown. Time to get back to the Keto diet for a bit!

Diet wasn't helped by my baking scones—again!—last weekend. I didn't mean to but Bill went to do some shopping for me and came back with buttermilk instead of cream. In a lame case for the defence, he pointed out that the two now come in the same coloured containers and how could he have known the difference? I could have said that that's what reading is for. *However*, I didn't, domestic harmony being a good thing. So I set out to use the stuff. I figured I might do better with scones than pancakes (why?) and lo! they were soft and light and delicious. I'd invited my sister Jane and brother-in-law Howard to afternoon tea, deliberately failing to remind them of my non-baking skills. I knew they'd be polite, and they were, but nevertheless declined my suggestion that they take the leftovers with them. Wise move. The next day they were like rocks and we could have played catch with them.

It's good to have the reassurance of community spirit and all the good things we need to prop ourselves up in difficult times. Something else occurred in recent days that meant that justice also is still with us; its long arm has not been lopped off. Back in the late 80s Bill was Ambassador to Mexico and the Central American republics. In that capacity, on a visit to El Salvador he called on the Jesuit rector of the Central American University. The rector, Ignacio Ellacuria, received him in his office, on the ground floor and with open windows, unusual given the dangerous times. The British Ambassador, Bill told the rector, had a heavily-guarded office without windows. "Well," was the reply, "we are in God's hands."

Within months, Ellacuria had been murdered, along with five other Jesuit priests, their housekeeper and her daughter, by government soldiers. It was an appalling act of murderous violence and the United States administration, which had been supporting the El Salvadoran government, immediately said "enough; this must change". And it did, but justice was not served in any but the most minor way. The high-level army officers escaped any trial. One former Salvadoran army colonel lived in the US for sixteen years until a federal judge in North Carolina approved his extradition to Spain in 2017. (Five of the priests were Spaniards.) Tried for the murders, this man has been sentenced to 133 years in prison. I remember Bill was shocked by those murders. Such a close encounter with goodness, only to see it brought down by evil. Let us hope that, at last, justice will be served.

Another profoundly impressive person from those El Salvador days was a pudgy determined ball of energy, Maria Julia Hernandez, director of a respected Catholic human rights agency. Directness was her stock in trade. When Bill offered her assistance from his human rights funds, she declined, saying that well-meaning Ambassadors only seemed to want to give her "office equipment and safe assistance"; what she needed was a four-wheel drive vehicle so she could go into the countryside and investigate reports of atrocities. Bill got the message; she got her wheels.

Moving on, I'm claiming grandmother bragging rights this week. Our grandson Charlie (our only grandson so we can logically say our favourite grandson) has just finished his first semester at university doing a business studies degree. Despite being new to university-style learning, and having to work at home with only computer contact with lecturers and tutors, Charlie has delivered the academic goods with style. We are, of course, as puffed up with pride as if we had done the courses ourselves. We suspect Charlie is following in his father's footsteps; Julian has moved through the banking sector and is now a partner in a financial advisory firm.

And so to this week's frivolity and another gem from Ben's book, *Ask the Past etc*, that I mentioned last week. Some advice from one Daniel of Beccles around 1200 on how to dress your child:

> Only cheap clothes should be given to little children. They smudge them with ashes, they stain them, they drool on them with their mouths, they wipe noses dripping with slime on their sleeves.

Charmant!

Have a happy week and keep safe.

With love

Elaine
15 June 2020

14
King of the Road

Dear Friends,

When it comes to reading I always have a night-time book on the go. It's what I reach for last thing at night for ten minutes or twenty, whatever I feel like. The main point about a night-time book is that it can go in one eye and out the other without rattling round much between. If I pick it up the next night and can't remember what I've read I flip back a page or two and am perfectly content to reread. These are not necessarily bad books; they're mostly jolly good yarns which don't tax a tired brain. At the moment, it's one of Kathy Reichs' forensic murder mysteries, *Death du Jour*. It refers to the smallpox epidemic in Montreal in the late 1880s and a nun who had tried to persuade church administrators to use isolation and immunisation to tackle the disease:

> She wrote to her bishop, pointing out that the fever was spread in places where crowds gathered, and begging him to temporarily close the church. Bishop Fabre refused, stating that to close the churches would be to laugh at God. The bishop urged his flock to church, telling them that united prayer was more powerful than prayer in isolation. Good thinking, Bishop. That's why French Catholics were dying and English Protestants were not. The heathens got inoculated and stayed home.

Well, well. One very clued-up nunny-bunny. This passage called to mind a couple of less than intelligent moments during the current pandemic when zealots, of a number of faiths, have beaten the faith-can-cure drum. Totally unhelpful. Like anti-vaxxers.

Lockdown is being eased in various ways throughout Australia and we can mostly be more mobile. So this week Bill and I took off with friends, Angus and Philippa, for a day in the country. This was no ordinary jaunt. You may recall I wrote about the massive hailstorm that smashed through Canberra in late January. Among the tens of thousands of cars damaged or destroyed was Angus's bright red VW sports coupé, a much-loved motor. Now it probably sits in one of the vast paddocks around Canberra where these cars are currently stored, weeping sadly over their fate. Angus, whose damaged and as yet unrepaired house roof is still covered by a tarpaulin, meaning a coldly grim winter for him, set about the business of acquiring a new car.

He has now unveiled for our admiring gaze a magnificent white 1983 Mercedes-Benz 230E of the W123 range. Angus tells us proudly that this car is among *das Beste vom Besten* of Mercedes-Benz. "Even so," I queried, "I thought you loved your VW coupé and would want another." "Ah yes," said Angus. "Yes, I did but that was a bit of a middle-aged man's fantasy. Now I want some dignity." And dignity this car has in spades. Angus is only the third owner of this beauty; it has been meticulously cared for and after thirty-seven years has only 40,000 kilometres on the clock. Hardly run in. Amusingly, the previous owner did not agree to sell it until he'd researched Angus. One has to be very careful about who owns such a car. Angus feels approved of!

So on Thursday we set out on our country adventure, for lunch at the pub in the tiny village of Wombat and afternoon tea in some other small country town. Of course, one does not ride in such a grand King of the Road without dressing for the occasion. We all dressed up, Bill and Angus looking frightfully smart in Harris tweed, Armani and ties; Philippa elegant in black and white, a lovely cream coat, and pearls. I'd thought the day would be cold so it would be heavy coats and trailing scarves and I could break out my fake fur hat and the whole adventure would be 'Zhivago goes to Wombat'. However, I didn't get to play Lara; it was a beautifully sunny day, chilly but not that chilly, so the hat didn't get an outing. I love this hat. As imitations go it is extremely good. Looks like mink and I enjoy seeing people's eyes pass lingeringly over it and the thought bubble floating above them, "goodness, she has a real fur hat". I don't bother disabusing them.

Now Wombat, you need to know, is so small you dare not blink or you really would miss it. It is a pub, two small houses, and a road in between. Even though it is so minute as to be almost non-existent, Wombat is typical of plenty of other Australian rural communities. They are recognisable by the friendliness of the locals, their strong sense of community, and a no-nonsense attitude that helps them through the toughest of times. Most of these communities are not fancy places but many attractive old buildings, large and small, remain as reminders of more vibrant days, times of gold rushes, or wheat or wool booms, when there was money, plenty of jobs and the young stayed around instead of disappearing as soon as they could to 'the big smoke' of, for example, Sydney or Melbourne.

Apart from having friendly and cheerful management, the Wombat pub is probably like a lot of American diners or Australian, English or New Zealand pubs in remote places where only the really hungry or thirsty stop, or those in the know about something special about the place. This pub is an ordinary, profoundly matter-of-face place, but it used to sell the most extraordinarily good meat pies made by a group of local women. For us, going there was always about buying a supply for the freezer. The ladies have given up their small business but the proprietor told us he's looking into reinstating this particular trade; a lot of people drove considerable distances for the Wombat Pub Pies. We'll certainly monitor this.

It was such a pleasure to see the countryside so green after the terrible summer we had and the long drought preceding it, now broken it seems. Everything is lush and the stock are as fat as butter. Farmers can regroup and rebuild, trying to put aside something again for the inevitable drought times of the future. That's life on the land in Australia. We rolled along, the Mercedes purring happily, exploring some of the lesser roads, and generally feeling free. "Bliss it was in that [time] to be alive", to misquote Wordsworth. We stopped in a tidy little town called Binalong where we set up in a little park for afternoon tea. Philippa had brought coffee and her delicious currant cake and I brought a basket with tablecloth, damask napkins, pretty plates and cutlery. And, naturally, a potted white cyclamen for the table. As one does for a picnic. Some local people saw all this and smiled broadly over the inanities of obvious city types.

I've looked up the figures and have discovered that, at the 2016 census, Wombat's population was 225, though goodness knows where they live. Tucked behind the surrounding hills I guess. At the same census, Binalong romped in with more than double the number; it teems with 543 residents. Like all these towns it has generously wide tree-lined streets, a centrally-placed war memorial, an old-fashioned two bowser petrol station, a grocery store, greengrocer and butcher. For me, the particular distinguishing feature of Binalong, through which I've driven many times, is something you would only see by accident. There is a signpost to a side road leading, the signpost's arrows inform us, to the Catholic church, the transfer station and the cemetery. It always amuses me so I look out for it, wondering each time how those who put it up missed the humour in it. Then again, maybe they didn't.

After our picnic we went into the local butcher's shop which proudly announces itself as "Lamboutique. Paris. Milan. Binalong". Such grandiosity is innocent enough; you see it everywhere but there is a special charm in such a tiny hamlet. The Binalong butcher's shop took me straight back to childhood and Strudwick's shop in Junee near where I grew up. Sawdust on the floor; large wooden butcher's blocks, scarred from years of cutting and carving; butchers in long navy and white striped aprons; and a very particular smell. In Binalong I closed my eyes and felt a child again, holding my mother's hand as she gave her order to the butcher. So we bought some of the Binalong butcher's prize-winning sausages and an enormous shoulder of lamb for a vast price. Why, you might well ask, and the only answer is the madness of the moment. Our friend Ada, whose many talents include a penchant for butchery, has since come round for dinner, bringing her knives, and has prepared it for roasting. It really is a huge shoulder; it's a moot point as to whether it came from a lamb or a hogget. We'll need quite a few friends to deal with it!

The rest of that bit of Wordsworth above is "but to be young was very heaven!" Sometimes you have to be in a sunshiny mood to agree with him, given the creaks and groans of advancing years. On the other hand, in our youth we were, my memory tells me, eager and keen to learn. The world was our oyster even if we didn't realise our parents' generation, and theirs *ad infinitum*, had thought the same thing. Certainly we felt immortal, invincible and all-wise but we also knew there really was much we didn't know. Things do seem a bit different now. Some of today's youth appear so certain, their thinking black and white, their passion not nuanced. The press this week spoke of a young British girl, a passionate activist, who, when asked what she thought of Winston Churchill, said, "Some people say he's a racist. I haven't personally met him."

What can one say? Such ignorance is hard to credit. Is it wilful? Lack of education? Was she trying to be funny? Or is such a remark the product of a social-media-driven mind closed to all but the comments of the like-minded on Facebook or Twitter or whatever? Having recovered from almost spilling our coffee when we came across this puzzling comment, Bill and I sat in stupefied silence, before laughing weakly and feeling old, Mr Wordsworth, old.

Let me hasten to add, I'm not trying to bag out the young. Age is not defining who's indulging in social bullying, confected outrage and an attempt to impose a unilaterally preferred shape on the present, and the future. I find it all singularly annoying because aggression and contorted thinking damage the credibility of genuine causes like freedom of speech, and tackling racism and discrimination. On which point, I wish the activists would not engage in reductionism by turning "Black Lives Matter" into BLM. The world has enough acronyms already which always have to be explained to some people. Let the cause speak for itself, loud and clear. Besides, BLM recalled to mind from childhood a horrible tonic called BCM which I'd successfully managed to forget. I can do without the two being confused.

And so to Ben's book again. You will recall last week's reference to the sometimes messy behaviour of children. A friend tells me one of her colleagues reported her three-year old as saying proudly, "Mummy, I didn't wipe my nose on my sleeve cos you said I shouldn't". Trouble was the child then grabbed Mummy's skirt. As I said last week, *charmant*. This time a tip from 1581. A gentleman called Thomas Hill, in his *Natural and Artificial Conclusions*, tells us how to walk on water:

> How to walke on the water. For to doe this, take two little Timbrels, and binde them vnder the soles of thy feete, and at a staues end fasten an other; and with these you maie safely walke on the water, vnto the wonder of all suche as shall see the same: if so be you often exercise the same with a certaine boldnesse and lightnesse of the bodie.

One hopes the righteous and the determinedly virtuous have sufficient humour to realise they are not Jesus.

Have a good week and keep safe.

With love

Elaine
22 June 2020

15
Indonesia & A Tale of COVID Loyalty

Dear Friends,

Bill and I go to Indonesia at least once a year. At least we have done since we left in 2010 (what happened to those ten years?) but coronavirus has put paid to all our 2020 travel plans. We are not permitted to travel abroad without special permission so our usual three Indonesian weeks in August/September will not happen this year. We have two places we always go. Two boutique hotels which are different but offer comfort, elegance and style.

The first, in Java, is Hotel d'Omah Jogjakarta which wanders through a little village called Tembi outside Jogjakarta like an elegant lady, embellishing her gardens with swimming pools, bar, cafe and lily ponds. The buildings borrow from the Javanese style of deep verandahs, high slanting tiled roofs and dim shady depths. Perfect for tropical Java and, given every room is air-conditioned, they become lovely cool caves where one can retreat from heat and humidity and lie about on comfortable giant beds under lazy ceiling fans, reading or doing absolutely nothing as one pleases, watching the *cicaks* (gekkos) chasing each other across the walls, calling *cicak-cicak* to each other as they go. Bliss.

D'Omah Tembi has a special history. It has been developed by our friend Warwick Purser, who is a remarkable expatriate Australian, but also an Indonesian citizen. He was accorded that rare honour of citizenship by sometime Indonesian President Susilo Bambang Yudhoyono in recognition of his decades of dedicated work turning Indonesian crafts into commercially viable and classy arts sold in high-end stores—like Neiman Marcus in New York—all over the world. Warwick is a designer whose creativity has built d'Omah into a lovely blend of Java and comfortable international style, using Indonesian batiks, paintings, statuary and *objets*.

We go to Tembi each August/September because the humidity drops then for the dry season. Humidity and I are not a happy mix given that I can't wear sandals, so the dry winter season at Tembi, plus air-conditioning, as opposed to the heat and humidity of the rest of the year, is my idea of heaven. I deserve it, I tell Bill, after having lived through four tropical postings—Fiji, Papua New Guinea, Malaysia and Indonesia. He says "no need to thank me; you're entirely welcome". So 'winter' in Tembi is my tropical option, especially as it gets us out of real winter in Canberra. Warm days with periodic downpours; lolling around with a good book in the *joglo* (open-sided sitting room) or on one's own terrace, thunder rolling round the skies, lightning flashing and forking, rain lashing the palm trees and stippling the swimming pools.

Then the nights. More bliss. Warm, soft, with humidity almost non-existent. The cliché of velvety nights warmly real. Always in the evening before dinner a visit to the bar by the lily pond and the orchid garden at the heart of the hotel, lights shining among the palm trees, where the charming Clemens brings us margaritas, gin-and-tonics or dry martinis. Very, very difficult to endure!

Of course, there is much more to do than our practice of 'absolutely nothing', aka recovery after the year's rigours of retirement. Jogjakarta is a very old cultural centre. There are temples, palaces, good restaurants, art galleries, markets, many art and craft shops and colonial Dutch buildings. Or one can take a lazy horse and buggy ride through the rice fields and nearby villages. Or simply stay home and play games in Warwick's studio, a showcase for his latest venture, Equatorial Design, a line of homewares, jewellery and beautiful modern batik fabrics and resort wear in soft silks, cottons and the very latest environmentally-friendly fabrics made from bamboo and even eucalyptus fibre.

The hotel nestles up to rice fields; early-morning walks offer more peaceful magical moments and always the question: will distant Mount Merapi be visible through the morning mist? Merapi is one of Indonesia's many active volcanoes and periodically belches lava and smoke from her depths. (Why she?) Walking with Warwick starts before six in the morning before the day's real heat but villagers are always about; cycling off to work or school, children scrubbed and tidy in super-clean uniforms; or old men and women sweeping the streets and yards as they do every day. Everyone is always friendly and enormously amused by the mad foreigners going for a walk. The children giggle and try out their English with *"hello, hello"*. Their parents and grandparents smile hugely saying, *"jalan jalan"* (walking). Walking in our gym gear for no discernible purpose is the source of great hilarity—especially about the men in shorts. Such a happy start to every day in Tembi.

This is Warwick's world. There he is now, in lockdown. We and all his friends have been concerned because Java is the most densely populated island in the world and it is hard to see how coronavirus would not run wild. Tembi's villagers decided very early on to lock down their village. They have set up barriers and 'no entry' signs at each entrance to the village; no non-villagers are allowed in. They have set up their own food system for the really poor and needy among them. This is Warwick's home but it is a challenging position to be in. He is not alone but there is no other good English speaker around. He speaks excellent Bahasa Indonesia but his English-speaking friends are in Bali or Jakarta and, of course, Canberra, but relations via telephone are no way the same as sitting together over coffee or a glass of wine, chatting and solving the world's problems.

Warwick could have left Tembi when lockdown seemed to be coming. He could have gone to Bali where he has a house and many friends, and where his daughter Polly lives with her husband Olivier and daughter Niluh. But he did not go. Coronavirus closed his hotel down as it cut a swathe through the tourist trade. He has stayed, caring for his hotel and few remaining staff. Doing exercise classes online and learning Javanese. But some staff have stayed with him—Freddy and Aziz, Ibnu, Nuri and Karno—and he, who could have left, has stayed with them. "How could I leave them?" he says. "They are sacrificing for me." This, for me and for Bill, is a great tale of the pandemic, a tale of loyalty, the kind of thing that is reassuring about the goodness of humankind, that across cultures there is a basic human understanding of what matters. Bill and I know Warwick's staff well; we are grateful to them for their kindness and loyalty to Warwick. It's loyalty beyond just a job, and grounded in something *we* might call a human universal but, somehow, for reasons that escape me, the post-modernists don't seem to believe in. Their loss.

Our other Indonesian go-to hotel is, like Warwick's, a contrast to the big glitzy tourist world. In Bali we stay at Bali Asri Villas in Seminyak where one walks down a cobbled walkway overhung with bougainvillea—a beautiful multi-coloured tunnel—with doorways periodically into private villas. Each villa has its own garden, pool, large open air sitting room and kitchen, huge bedroom and dressing room plus an indoor/outdoor bathroom. Showering under an open sky surrounded by rock gardens, ferns and elegance is matched only by the fact that each villa has a butler who comes at a phone call to cook meals, make drinks, deliver a pizza or just take care of the laundry. More bliss. Being in a Bali Asri Villa is to retreat into a private domain where the world and its woes do not exist. It's the creation of its owners and our valued friends Made, who is Balinese, and his French partner, Jean Pierre, so is a lovely blend of styles and a beautiful contrast to the marble and glitz world, not far from its doors, of big resorts and hotel chains, streets of high-end fashion shops, spas, bars and fancy restaurants.

In lieu of lovely sloth in Tembi and Bali, we must now content ourselves with short forays out of Canberra. Even they might be curtailed if the current outbreak of COVID19 cases in Melbourne forces renewed lockdown. This weekend we went to our daughter Catherine's for granddaughter Tess's sixteenth birthday party. Great fun and a delight to see the young ones growing up with such poise and style. I had neither at sixteen so get a real buzz from seeing it shaping up for the future. Before Catherine's in Stanwell Park we got away to a magical place not far from her, the small town of Bundeena just south of Sydney, squeezed in between the sea and the Royal National Park which was established in 1879, making it Australia's oldest, and the world's third oldest, national park. Our friend Robbie was staying in a house belonging to friends of hers when lockdown came and has now been there for four months. Her partner, Robin, had had to leave (yes, they do have the same name!) so unfortunately we missed him but it was still a great catch-up with a terrific dinner and lots of laughter. The house's garden wanders down a steep incline to a tiny beach, all rock shelves and hard-packed sand (the kind I can walk on), and faces west so we had the gift of a magnificent sunset. Neither of us had been to Bundeena before; a great discovery.

Speaking of small places, you will recall last week I wrote about that minute village of Wombat.

I've had a number of responses suggesting it's quite well known. Ben, he-of-the-book I've quoted from over the past few weeks, tells me he went to law school with someone from Wombat. A priest friend, Harvey, wrote reminding me he'd been principal (!) of the one-teacher school at "the Bat" while another of our colleagues, Simon, reminded me that a bishop of the Anglican Diocese of Canberra and Goulburn once went to the Wombat pub, taking a break on the long drive between engagements. He was in clerical dress and you can imagine the silence that fell when the locals saw this man in full episcopal regalia. The bishop was more than up to the moment. "Right," he said, "I'll buy a beer for anyone who's willing to talk to me." I imagine he had quite a few takers. Now that's evangelism.

And so to Ben's book . . . a little advice from 1579 on how to avoid the plague:

> Whosoeuer eateth two Walnuts, fwo Fygs, twenty leaues of Rew, and one graine of Salt, all stampt and mixt together, fasting: shall bee safe from poyson and plague that daye.

Apparently, Ecclesiastes got it right and there really is nothing new under the sun. Sounds like a slushy to me. Be that as it may, as the book suggests, I'd take it with a grain of salt.

With love and stay safe

Elaine
29 June 2020

16
No Partridges in Our Pear Tree

Dear Friends

> 4 hammers, 1 sledgehammer, 1 mallet, 3 files, 6 pliers, 8 shifting spanners, 4 wire brushes, 5 boxes of nails, tacks and screws, 16 tins of paint, 19 screwdrivers, 16 paintbrushes, 4 tins of WD40, 3 tape measures, 4 garden brooms, 3 shovels, 4 handsaws, 2 hacksaws and 1 *huge* crowbar

Bill has been clearing out our garden shed. A crowbar? Who on earth needs a crowbar in a moderately-sized domestic garden? We actually don't remember why we have it but we know it was my father's from the farm of my youth. It will find a new home with Mick, our landscape garden design friend, who, among other advantages, has the strength to lift it. As well as the above, sundry other items emerged: a vast assortment of rope, string and garden ties, wooden or bamboo garden stakes, bits of shade cloth and sheets of plastic, not to mention old bedsheets and curtains for use as painting drop-sheets.

The garden shed clear-out was brought on partly because of lockdown, partly because of January's hailstorm damage to the shed, and partly because it seemed a good idea at the time when the thought of a clear-up struck. The shed has now been reduced to an order and tidiness that rival even my reorganised kitchen drawers. An incredible achievement because Bill isn't the manic neatness freak that I have become, demanding symmetry and precision in all around me. Which means I live in a regular state of disappointment! I'm about to attack bathroom cabinets because I think I need another burst of order.

Meanwhile Bill has attacked the task of restoring our three garden benches, which are wobbly and rusted, with some of the wood rotted, broken or missing. We looked for replacements but both had an attack of niggardliness, if there is such a word. So restoration began. Every now and again I have to go out for what we call "ooh-aah" moments, and dish up words of wonder and admiration. So far one bench has been scraped down, derusted, scrubbed, painted with anti-rust, anti-mould, anti-various-other-things and painted afresh. Elegant black metal work and dark brown wooden seat. The other two are receiving similar treatment but I suspect enthusiasm is beginning to ebb because I'm being told not to look too hard.

These seats are for the downside of our garden. The garbage bin side with the tool shed at one end. And where the BBQ stands. Now it's confession time. You need to know that we are probably the only two Australians who have removed a built-in BBQ from a property— our last house. It's essentially un-Australian to do so; basically national blasphemy or sacrilege. Everyone has a BBQ. Everyone uses a BBQ a couple of times a week. Not us. At least we do have a BBQ. We bought it before we went to Jakarta at the insistence of our son, Julian, who told us about a special on at some shop and intimated we should buy one because the BBQ on sale was called *Garth* which is our son-in-law's name. Julian insisted, "Dad, do the right thing and get yourself a BBQ". So we bought the *Garth* in 2004 but didn't actually get round to buying a gas bottle till 2018. Not that we used it even then. The gas bottle sat lonely and forlorn in the corner of the garage until last spring.

And a day when all the family came round including our young Mexican 'honorary children', Pierre and Karla. They came to Australia four years ago to study, work and pursue Australian citizenship. They now have permanent residency and are awaiting the big day for citizenship. They are young, eager, dedicated and determined to become Australian. Pierre took matters in hand. He cleaned the BBQ. He set it up and lo! it worked. Pierre, Julian and Garth also cooked which was even better. And cleaned the BBQ afterwards. Sadly, we are so slack that we haven't used it since. We mean to but are so unaccustomed to thinking about barbecuing that we never do. We could try to wriggle out of this by saying BBQs are banned during summers like the last horror season but that's no excuse. All we can do is say lamely, "We don't barbecue". I guess we're waiting for our Mexican/Australian friends to come and visit again. Pierre and Karla, you are under orders!

Meantime, the pandemic rages on. Except for the outbreak in Melbourne and renewed strict lockdown in some areas there, restrictions for the rest of us are easing. This has, among other things, included the re-opening of our gym and our resumption of rising at stupid o'clock to get gym out of the way early. But whatever normal was, it is not returning. Most people continue to be extremely careful and vigilant. My life seems centred on my computer, churning out various papers and, of course, this weekly letter. I have been writing to you now for sixteen weeks and my reasons remain the same. Friendship is absolutely at the heart of my thinking. We cannot travel overseas. We cannot yet travel freely within Australia. You, our friends, are all over the place and we miss you. Zoom doesn't seem to work on my computer—at least I could see and hear but no one on the other end could see or hear me so I gave up.

But now I have a beautiful snippet to listen to first thing each morning. A video of our New York friend, Peter Argondizza, who is a classical guitarist. You may recall my writing about Peter and Carol's postponed wedding on 25 April. Last summer we were all together in Sag Harbor on Long Island for a few happy days with mutual friends, Susan and Robert. Part of that precious time was our own in-house concert with Peter entertaining us. Anyone out there interested in guitar should go online and learn about his online concerts and master classes. By the way, Peter has been recording with Yo Yo Ma so Peter's another Mr Golden Fingers!

In the meantime, I will continue writing. I enjoy time thinking of you all each week. These letters have been the happy side of trying to be disciplined during an abnormal time when it is quite easy to dither around. We've not been too bad about our lockdown goal of clearing out books but I admit I've lost patience with more books and been more critical than I usually am. There have been some good finds and the following poem is one I want to share. I've been reading Malcolm Guite's work for some time now, liking it immensely, and finding it very useful for sermons. A priest who appreciates the poetry in life rather than huddling behind hard-edged rules is a great find. Guite is English, a Church of England priest, a poet, an academic, a singer, Chaplain at Girton College, Cambridge, plays with a rock band and looks like a delightful Hobbit. I am in awe of his versatility and virtuosity. This poem *Because We Hunkered Down* seems to fit our difficult times so well, despite its differences in time and climate:

These bleak and freezing seasons may mean grace
When they are memory. In time to come
When we speak truth, then they will have their place,
Telling the story of our journey home,
Through dark December and stark January
With all its disappointments, through the murk
And dreariness of frozen February,
When even breathing seemed unwelcome work.

Because through all of these we held together,
Because we shunned the impulse to let go,
Because we hunkered down through our dark weather,
And trusted to the soil beneath the snow,
Slowly, slowly, turning a cold key,
Spring will unlock our hearts and set us free.

And so to Ben's book and advice on how to cure a sore throat from 1685 and Nicolas Lemery's work *Modern Curiosities of Art & Nature:*

Take a Sheeps small Guts, put them about your Neck till they be cold; then apply others hot, from the Sheep new Kill'd, and so continue this as long as you please.

With apologies to Master Lemery, I please not.

With love and keep safe

Elaine
6 July 2020

17
Living in Books

Dear Friends,

The weather has been beautifully sunny during the past week and one afternoon I found Bill in the garden surrounded by shoes. "Do many people still shine shoes?" he asked. "Probably not a lot," I suggested. Then, remembering we'd watched *A Tale of Two Cities* a few nights before, I added "are you trying to make like Dr Manette?" "Ah-oui," was the reply in his best Inspector Clouseau French and he added that, as a reward, he would like some fruit Bastilles. Ignoring this, I pointed out that Dr Manette didn't shine shoes, he cobbled, and I wandered off leaving him to his (and my!) shoes. *A Tale of Two Cities*. Oh goodness! Read in teenage years full of angst, insecurity and self-conscious blushes. Such romance, danger, love, sacrifice. I remember weeping over it as Sydney Carton mounted the guillotine. "It is a far, far better thing that I do, than I have ever done; it is a far, far better rest that I go to than I have ever known." Oh my God, I'd wailed to myself. Will there ever be a Sydney Carton for me? I got over myself in time. Maybe.

Last week I said I'd been impatient with more books than usual during these months but I've done better this week. I discovered a book I didn't even know we had, *The Dinner Party*, by Howard Fast and published in 1987. Not an author I've read and neither of us knows how we came by this slim volume but I need to tell you it won't be going on the reject pile. The title interested immediately given the life we've led, and on page four I found a remark confirming that interest, that a proper and successful dinner party is a work of art. Fast had his character say, "it has always been that as long as civilisation has been around, but most hostesses don't give a moment's thought to the dinner party as an art form".

Well this hostess did—and does. In the beginning, it wasn't intentional, more a question of survival; life seemed to have tipped me into the diplomatic world and I needed to get on top of it. It didn't take long to work out that, if you can't cook—and I couldn't— you'd best learn. In the meantime, I had to trust that you can fool most people most of the time with minced meat if you present it appealingly. But year flowed into year of doing this, and the lack of viable alternatives, like a job of my own, began to bother. Still, like diplomatic wives before me, and quite a few since, I followed along, from country to country, doing the right thing but not finding an answer to the question, "is this all there is?"

All the same, in many ways it was a good and interesting life. It fitted the opening lines of *A Tale of Two Cities:* "it was the best of times, it was the worst of times". So, like all those other women, I got on with it and did the best I could with "the dinner party as an art form". But that question—is this all there is?—hovered in the background, even if mostly silenced. One day it hit me forcibly and would no longer remain silent. It was 1995. I was sitting alone in Brisbane airport waiting for a plane back to Port Moresby. For a now forgotten reason I was in an excellent mood and wearing a cream jacket I loved with a big brown silk rose on the lapel. Not exactly normal attire for a plane trip nor for the relaxed world of Papua New Guinea but I didn't care. I felt terrific and all was exceptionally well with the world as I sat waiting and reading Jane Gardam's 1991 book, *The Queen of the Tambourine* about a British Foreign Office wife looking at her life, trying to make sense of her past for the sake of her future. Her marriage had failed and someone suggested she find a job. She replied:

> I had a job. For thirty years I had Henry . . . When we married it was made quite clear to me that Henry's job in the Foreign Service was shared between us. Diplomatic wives were not allowed any other work then. It's different now. Then it was full-time social punishment and doing the intellectual and diplomatic polite. We were Oxbridge-trained geisha girls and I was a very good one. And I was worth something better.

I burst into tears in the airport lounge. There was a good deal of uncomfortable shifting around me, people's eyes sliding in any direction but towards me. I sobbed messily for a few moments about this bit of my life on the page! I got the bewilderment and the sense of a life spent staring through a window, of being lost on the edge of a world, someone else's world, caught up in that world, honouring it but wanting more. Do we all have these moments when we discover ourselves in books? It's confronting but you have to pull yourself together. In my case, I'm a blotchy weeper, which is not a good look so my usual practice is to wipe my eyes, reach for Post-it notes and start littering yet another book, marking something I want to remember and revisit from time to time.

Now here I am today, twenty-five years later, with no idea how many dinners and other events I've organised, and I've discovered myself in another book in another writer's words. The hostess in Howard Fast's book, a wealthy woman in her own right (unlike me!), is the wife of an American Democrat senator and is fine-tuning arrangements for an important dinner:

> All her life she had been exposed to the conversation—better called chatter—of the rich and powerful, and unless it dealt directly with the business of being rich and exercising power, it was filled with inanities; and since their women were excluded for the most part from the business of getting richer or increasing power, they spoke of little else other than inanities. Never had she heard, in the chatter over cocktails and across dinner tables, philosophy, personal or otherwise; curiosity concerning the universe and its ultimate mysteries; thoughts, however, puerile, about the fate or hopes of man; points of ethics or hints of brotherhood. Yes, books, when they were marked as best sellers by the *Washington Post*, films and plays occasionally, but without depth and without wit. Long ago, she had ceased to be a participant and had become an observer.

Life as an observer. Interesting thought, not new to me, and I can assure you it develops skills. There are plenty of people who like the sound of their own voices: politicians and ministers pursuing their particular briefs and/or party interests; diplomats circling their national interests with careful words; wine snobs who spoil the wine with self-important pontificating; wine bibbers whose tipsy tongues run away with them; academics carried away by their own eloquence. My list is quite long and I'm sure you have your own. No one who knows me would imagine I would stay silent in many circumstances but, faced with any of the above, it's sometimes worth it. You listen, you watch, you read faces, gestures, body language. You gauge and judge. You can occasionally pick up nuances that watchers see more readily than the speakers. If you set your mind to it, being an observer is an interesting pastime, and productive. I've more than once reported to Bill the flutter of a hand, a dropped glance, or a tensed foot that has contradicted words and smiles. It's been fun. The games people play . . .

But there's more to it than that. At least there has been for me. After that day at Brisbane airport with Gardam's book I set out to plot a different course. I would not rebuild old defences against the world. Of course, we all have a few defences—we need them—but nothing too high and set in stone, and no using old stones from broken-down defences. Instead I would build 'new being'. Mind you, we all know we don't say things like that and then just do them. Time, a lifetime, and a bit of effort do the trick. And the job is never really finished. For me, hostess and observer blended gradually but happily and the key was realising and pursuing what Dickens' character Sydney Carton demonstrated. Dickens may have been a pretty awful piece of work (read the chapter in Phyllis Rose's *Parallel Lives* on the way he treated his wife) but he was a fine reader of character and human nature and shone stark unsettling spotlights on the social ills of his country and culture.

Dickens used Sydney Carton to show sacrifice as gift to another person and not gain for oneself. It seems so simple but it's somehow counter-intuitive for mere mortals. We stuff it up all the time. Those of you who are Christian will recognise in this definition of sacrifice the fundamental message of the Christ figure. Which is exactly why I was gradually able to pull the bits of my world together. Jane Gardam and Howard Fast alive in my world! Diplomat's wife and priest met and became one over meals—at the dinner table and the altar. That's the 'new being'. Not that that's the end of the matter. In the process, I realised that there was a Sydney Carton for me. Fifty-one years of marriage and a helluva lot of experiences, good and bad, and recognising a figure of humility and sacrifice quite close at hand. Sydney Carton had simply changed his name to Bill.

I'm not being sentimental. I love the idealistic dreams of the young if not their current methods but I sometimes fear they don't realise that the world is messy and life just sucks at times. I guess we were the same in our youth! Whatever we think love is when we're twenty-one, it's a damned sight better when we're older, having learned to accept mess, broken dreams, different paths, different goals, and to enjoy subtleties and nuances. Thank you, Bill. Including for the shiny shoes.

Now in past weeks I've offered you amusing snippets from Ben's book but I'm going to have to return it to him. Borrowing books is a dangerous thing, especially when you enjoy them. I have fifteen Post-it notes to remove this time! For this week, one I thought rather apt in these germy days: advice from a 1777 source, *The Complete Vermin-Killer*, on how to kill bedbugs:

> Spread Gun-powder, beaten small, about the crevices of your
> bedstead; fire it with a match, and keep the smoke in; do this
> for an hour or more, and keep the room close several hours.

Good luck with that one. Guy Fawkes only tried to blow up the British parliament. Take the vermin-killer's advice and you'll do for the neighbourhood. Next week we'll farewell Ben's book with a little sage advice on how to prevent drunkenness. We can all drink to that. In the meantime, I have a dinner party to prepare. I'm off to make pinot noir biscuits to serve with anchovy mousse. There are more ways than one to take one's wine.

Take care and keep safe

With love

Elaine
13 July 2020

PS. Oh, by the way, Bill has done a stocktake of HIS shoes: 5 brown leather, 7 black leather, 10 suede (1 black, 4 brown, 1 red, 1 green, and 3 blue), 1 pair of sandals, 2 pairs of sandshoes, 2 pairs of sneakers and 2 crocs. I didn't know he had such a thing about shoes. He points out a little tartly I have no shoes to stand in (so to speak) in this debate, as I'd be the one getting the Imelda Award. I'm not saying a thing.

18
Birthdays and Bulbs

Dear Friends,

Those of us who live in Canberra know one of its secrets. Glorious winter days. Of course we do get dismal grey rainy days but often winter here means blue cloudless skies and a brisk chill whose edges are softened by bright sun. Plenty of people from Sydney and Melbourne like to scoff at Canberra, calling it a dull, charmless and isolated political bubble, but that seems driven more by casually familiar empty rhetoric than real knowledge. This is a really easy and comfortable place to live and, in these coronavirus times, many of us who have been a bit slack before are discovering an extensive network of walking paths, many carefully maintained through parks and around lakes, others left rocky and rugged through nature reserves. As national capitals go, Canberra is interesting: groups of suburbs sprawl their way around hills and bushland rather than covering everything in sight with concrete and bricks. Going walking is the thing-of-the-moment and plenty of people who haven't exercised systematically before have started to push themselves, exercise being one of the few excuses to be out and about during lockdown.

On Friday Jennifer and I took our Nordic walking poles and walked for a couple of hours in one of these chunks of bushland in the middle of suburbs. Our path took us up a steep rough slope then round a hill giving splendid views. Canberra is largely surrounded by mountains and yesterday they were clear and purple in the sunshine. Well, we call them mountains; others with real mountains, like New Zealanders and the Swiss, for example, would call them mere hills! Every ridge and treetop seemed to stand out and round us wattle trees were in bright yellow glory—the Cootamundra, the first of the wattle season. Flocks of harshly squawking sulphur-crested cockatoos were busy and bold as they fed among the trees, their great white bodies looking so sleek they were obviously finding plenty to eat. An English tourist once commented about these particular cockatoos: "English birds are so much quieter. They just tweet and twitter. These Australian birds are like a bunch of raucous football hooligans!"

Less common than the sulphur-crested cockatoo is the gang-gang and I saw a flight of them hanging out together, enjoying the day. The gang-gang is also a cockatoo. The male has a scarlet red head and crest, with the rest of the body slate-grey; the female's head is dark grey, with pink- and yellow- edged feathers under its body. Just another of Australia's unusual and brilliantly-coloured birds. Overseas visitors are regularly astonished by their vibrancy after the more sober bird life often encountered elsewhere.

Halfway up the hill we turned a corner and came face to face with one of Australia's national emblems, a kangaroo. Fortunately, not the other emblem—the emu—which is a rather cranky bird and can be quite aggressive. The kangaroo wasn't at all put out by our sudden invasion of its territory; just stood there, staring at us and twitching its ears. We apologised for not being able to twitch ours back by way of polite conversation but oohed and aahed at it instead, thinking how lovely to live somewhere where kangaroos abound. Every dry season they invade the city in search of food and water and it's not uncommon to find one nibbling in one's garden or hopping across the road in front of the car. You have to be very careful in the early mornings or evenings; care or no, road kill is pretty common. On the other hand, living here we know places where we can go for a quiet evening drink and watch dozens of them feeding or bounding by.

Meanwhile, anxiety still rules. We wait for possible renewed lockdown as new outbreaks occur in Melbourne and Sydney. The numbers are minute in comparison with the US, Mexico and Brazil, for example, but only because of the strict measures that have been taken, and we may well see such measures again. There was fear this week that Melbourne's cases had increased because of the protests some weeks back in support of the Black Lives Matter movement but that has not been proven. A great cause, though I am troubled by some of the methods and the idea that anger alone can change things overnight. Anger needs direction to carry people with you for your cause. I am conscious that I'm writing this on Saturday 18th July, the anniversary of Nelson Mandela's birth in 1918. Now there was a great man, a worthy hero for anyone. "Don't judge me by my successes," he said, "judge me by how many times I fell down and got back up again." And he refused to allow portraits of South Africa's Apartheid-era leaders to be removed from their parliament house. Remember your history and learn from it. Hear, hear!

Moving on to another form of history, my friend Robert in the US turns 60 in a few days. So young and so fresh! I've suggested to him that he greet this milestone with pleasure and anticipate the years to come with glee. They're OK! I remember my 60th. We were still in Jakarta and I was not looking forward to my birthday with any pleasure. None of the earlier milestones had bothered me but turning 60 was the pits. Some days before I happened to be talking to Robin, Bill's wonderful Personal Assistant, when gloom flattened me and I burst into tears, wailing about no career and no time left and woe is me. Embarrassing. Robin was unfazed. I learned later that she knocked on Bill's door and said, "Ambassador, may I speak with you a moment?" Invited in, she then closed the door and said, "Bill, go home! Elaine's having a meltdown over turning 60!" Bill obeyed, came home and took me somewhere swanky for lunch.

On the day itself we were at Warwick's hotel, d'Omah Jogjakarta that I wrote about a couple of weeks back. Bill had work to do; calling on the Sultan of Jogjakarta and sundry others to discuss this and that. I hung out with Warwick. Bill claims he called in several times during the day and found us with large goldfish bowls of cold white wine in our hands but he's making it up. It was only once! In fact, Warwick took me to browse in Moesson's antique store. It's run by Wym, a man from a Dutch family which stayed on after Indonesia gained independence from the Netherlands. He sells a fascinating range of genuine antiques and the manufactured antiqued variety of bric-a-brac but he's upfront about which is which. That was the day I saw IT: a lovely large three-storey dolls' house. It was pre-independence, modelled on a Dutch house, and had belonged to a Dutch family. There was a slight, determined but polite tussle between Warwick and me as to who was going to buy it and I won. In fact, Warwick, dear man, probably simply demurred in honour of my birthday. Or maybe I have sharper elbows.

Anyway, that's what you do on your 60th birthday: you buy a dolls' house or something else that you love and absolutely do not have to have. I told myself it was for the grandchildren to play with but it wasn't true; it was for me and I was amused one day in Canberra when a plumber asked me after he'd done whatever if he could look at it. He turned out to be a member of Canberra's dolls' house association! Who knew there is one? In Jakarta, I put it on a cabinet outside the dining room and it was touching how quickly the staff took to putting minute bowls of tuber rose blossoms on its tables! I also noticed clusters of guests pausing on their way in to dinner and gently fingering this or that tiny chair or cabinet. There are ways and ways of putting one's guests in a good mood.

Oh, I have another comment on dinner parties and hospitality for you. Rob et Catherine wrote from France reminding me of Cardinal John Henry Newman's words about company which are easily applicable to dinner parties: "The true gentleman [or gentlewoman, we three think] has eyes on all his company; he is tender towards the bashful, gentle towards the distant, and merciful towards the absurd; he can recollect to whom he is speaking; he guards against unseasonable allusions, or topics which may irritate; he is seldom prominent in conversation, and never wearisome". So there.

So, Robert, as I've already said to you, I know many would think me nuts to say so but the post-60th years are just fine. Think old wine and be happy. As well as drinking the wine. As opposed to spilling it as Bill did at my 21st birthday party a thousand years ago. We were in his university college rooms along with about a dozen or so friends. There was a heated debate about some political point and Bill, who was seated on the arm of my chair forgot himself, gesticulating wildly with his glass of red wine in hand. I was wearing a beautiful NEW white wool suit. Vale, suit. I forgave him eventually. Eventually.

All this sunshine, wattle and even the odd blossom tree sprouting brings on thoughts of spring, which is still a way off, but spring means bulbs. I need to report a moderate success in the matter of bulbs of which I am a little bit proud. For years I have been meaning to grow hyacinths in bowls for the house in spring and for years I've never remembered to plant the bulbs in time. This year I remembered, if not quite on time. In preparation for this exercise I bought pretty pots (why when I have plenty of serviceable ones to use?) and special bulb potting mix. I put the prepared bowls in the light of the kitchen window and fed and watered the things assiduously. Lo! the bulbs have sprouted and some are even flowering. A lovely rich purpley-blue. Actually that was a bit of a surprise. I'd thought I'd bought white but, not a problem; if they'd produced pink flowers, of which I am not fond, I might have ripped them up.

But there they are. I found myself remembering E.M. Delafield and her wonderful *Diary of a Provincial Lady*. Delafield was extremely popular on both sides of the Atlantic in the 1930s and 40s with her witty, ironic, slightly self-deprecatory diaries. They're very English and dated here and there but her sharp eye and clever turn of phrase as she quietly dissects characters around her are as freshly applicable to people we know in our own lives as they were in her day. The bane of the provincial lady's existence was Lady Boxe, the local *grande dame* in her English village. *Diary of a Provincial Lady* opens with her observation:

> *November 7th.* Plant the indoor bulbs. Just as I am in the middle of them, Lady Boxe calls. I say, untruthfully, how nice to see her, and beg her to sit down while I just finish the bulbs. Lady B. makes determined attempt to sit down in armchair where I have already placed two bulb-bowls and the bag of charcoal, is headed off just in time, and takes the sofa. Do I know, she asks, how very late it is for indoor bulbs? September, really, or even October, is the time. Do I know that the only really reliable firm for hyacinths is Somebody of Haarlem? Cannot catch the name of the firm, which is Dutch, but reply Yes, I do know, but think it my duty to buy Empire products. Feel at the time, and still think, that this is an excellent reply. Unfortunately Vicky [daughter] comes into the drawing-room later and says: "Oh, Mummie, are those the bulbs we got at Woolworth's?"

Well, transplanting the seasons, I was only about a month late planting my bulbs but fortunately nobody has told me so. That being said, we've all known the Lady Boxe type who simply must tell you what you do not want to be told and we can feel for the provincial lady who maintains her outward cool at least whilst seething inside and wishing she could poke the woman's eyes out. As for my bulbs, I had fantasies of great lush flower heads which I could thrust at people to admire but I haven't quite got the dream. Three have flowered in a spindly sort of way, two look as if they are thinking about it, and two are being recalcitrant. Better luck next year and I shall mark my diary and hope I remember to look at the entry.

And now the final piece I promised from Ben's book. A little advice from one Hugh Plat, in *The Jewel House of Art and Nature* of 1653:

> How to prevent drunkenness. Drink first a good large draught of Sallet Oyl, for that will float upon the Wine which you shall drink, and suppress the spirits from ascending into the brain. Also what quantity soever of new milk you drink first, you may well drink thrise as much wine after, without danger of being drunk. But how sick you shal be with this prevention, I wil not here determine.

Nor will I. The editor of Ben's book suggests: "the recipe for a foolproof anti-drunkenness cocktail: three parts wine, one part milk, a dash of salad oil. Shake well and immediately reconsider". I will definitely do so and recommend a similar policy to Robert as he celebrates his 60th!

Take care and keep safe

With love

Elaine
20 July 2020

19
Don't Call Me Dearest!

Dear Friends,

What's in a word? A great deal, especially the word *dearest*. In this household, I maintain this word's a ploy Bill resorts to when negotiations have reached an impasse. Neither of us going to give in and, in response to another sally from me, then comes the grin, and "yes, dearest", followed by "no, dearest" and on it goes. I know this "dearest" ploy well. I say it translates into "I'm right and you're wrong, and who's going to give in first?!" and Bill just grins. It's infuriating and I get huffy and shriek "don't call me dearest!" Or wish I'd thought of borrowing from Dorothy Parker and yelling, "Don't look at me in that tone of voice!" Tempted to juvenile foot-stamping, I snap crossly that he reminds me of the awful little brother in the film *Sixteen Candles* and when do grown men grow out of teasing? For those of you who haven't seen *Sixteen Candles* it's a romantic piece of filmic fluff. We watched it again recently with Tess on her sixteenth birthday. Great for a laugh and a cringe here and there but, unless you want that and a bit of escapism, don't rush to Netflix. It's a film more for ritual moments than movie appreciation.

Of course, domestic relations are always (eventually!) resumed and we find our way out of the impasse. You don't stay married as long as we have unless you can climb mountains and skirt potholes along the way. And cede territory (with ever so much graciousness) or accept victory (ditto) and live to spar again. One of the weird things about long relationships is how thought patterns coalesce unexpectedly. We can be quietly reading, or driving somewhere in silence, or just pottering at home, when one of us says something which brings the other to a sudden standstill (difficult when you're the driver). "I was just thinking that!" is the astonished outcry. These days we simply say "too long", which is shorthand for "we've been married too long". I guess it's a version of the old claim that long-married people begin to look like each other (better than looking like their dogs—usually). I know my handwriting lurched dangerously towards Bill's script a while ago which raised an alarm for me. My writing's better than his! Not wanting to be subsumed, I'm taking care.

Obviously, it isn't just couples who develop sayings and special words. Families do a similar thing. In our family, "Hi Mum!" is a familiar one. It's an abbreviation of "Hi Mum! I'd like you to meet etc" from the days when our daughter brought home friends we parents thought awful and quite unsuitable! She hated it; now it just elicits a wry smile. With Julian it was different; he and Jessica simply bonded and were known as "the married couple" pretty much from the beginning! More recently, we had a fun expression for speaking before one thinks: "it's a thought, Mimi". When granddaughter Mimi was a little girl, words and thoughts sometimes tumbled out of her mouth so quickly she'd get tied up in knots. Then she'd laugh, a loud shout of laughter, and we'd join her saying, "it's a thought, Mimi". But we don't use the expression at the moment. Mimi's fourteen and we're all a bit nervous about that self-conscious stage. We'll leave it till she's older and will appreciate once more the affection in the phrase. Teasing, yes, but wrapped around with love—and not a negotiation in sight!

But what to say instead? My friend Sarah and I were musing on this recently while out walking. Admittedly, we were thinking in a rather different context, less about affection and more about making a point. As when you secretly want to poke someone's eyes out. I think I must be getting bitter and twisted; this is the second week in a row I've talked about doing that. Blame it on the pandemic; it's the current catch-all excuse and useful to boot. Be that as it may, Sarah and I settled on the expression "did you mean to say that out loud?" Not bad as putdowns go but there's just a touch of plaintive hopefulness about it. It's dependent upon the other person's detecting the barb without sensing the plea.

By far the most delicious putdown I've come across, and one I'd love to have the *chutzpah* to use at times, was in *Shadowlands*, the film about American poet Joy Davidman and C. S. Lewis starring Anthony Hopkins and Debra Winger. Do you remember the scene? Lewis introduces his new wife to his academic colleagues at dinner at his Oxford college. One man treats Davidman with awful condescension at which she smiles broadly, and says with deceptive sweetness, "Perhaps there is a cultural difference here but I don't quite understand. Are you trying to be offensive or are you merely stupid?" Ouch! Yes! Whoever dreamed that up has a fine sense for pure nastiness. We need such people to think up these lines for us. Even if we never say them out loud we can fantasise at will (or, in my case, at Bill), and cast borrowed barbs at those we'd love to bring down. But out loud, so to speak, go on smiling sweetly.

By the way, *Shadowlands* is an absolute must. No fluff about it at all. An old film but wonderful and it's on Netflix and probably on any number of other websites. Which reminds me, I wrote about Canberra last week and what an attractive place it is. For some stunning photography and a little mild entertainment at the same time watch the Australian TV series *Secret City*. It too is on Netflix (what isn't?). The story involves politicians, spies, journalists, murders and Sino-Australian relations (how very of-the-moment!) in a crazy and unbelievable mix. It's worth watching for two things: the photography and the performance of Australian actor Jackie Weaver. She plays a malign, malicious, take-no-prisoners Australian Attorney-General who gets low down and dirty with anyone who crosses her. It is said that Barack Obama watched and loved *Secret City*, so much so that he rang Jackie Weaver to commend her on her acting. Apparently nastiness can win plaudits.

Back to 'the cut direct'. The best I've managed was a riposte to a man complaining that a mutual acquaintance with whom he was seated at dinner was dull and never said boo. He, an arrogant bore and bighead, was referring to a cultured and clever woman. I suggested that if she'd been silent it might have had something to do with the company. Three out of ten at best.

For me, the mistress of wit and wordplay is Dorothy Parker, the master Oscar Wilde. I know there are many others. Clive James and Erma Bombeck are old favourites, all of them among my *crème de la crème* of witty writers. I sit at their feet, silent with admiration (except for laughing) and too awed to envy. They play with words, making them shock as well as ring with fun. And in the middle of their play what they say is not just funny but clever and suddenly blindingly obvious. I think sometimes of the tortured figure of Salieri in the film *Amadeus*, torn with envy turned to hatred over the brilliance of Mozart—"Oh God, how could you give him so much?" In other words, why could I not have a little more? But I don't play Salieri. I just revel in minds like Wilde's talking about a widow whose hair had gone quite gold with grief, or that a good friend will always stab you in the front. Or like Parker's pointing out that brevity is the soul of lingerie; and that famous line that you can lead a horticulture, but you can't make her think. I imagine you all know that equally famous verse attributed to Parker, possibly wrongly:

> I like to have a martini,
> Two at the very most.
> After three I'm under the table,
> after four I'm under my host.

Interestingly, like so many in whom the comedic gifts were strong, Parker and Wilde knew more than a bit about life's underbelly. "What fresh hell is this?" agonised Parker. Wilde had one of his characters in *Lady Windermere's Fan* say, "we are all in the gutter, but some of us are looking at the stars". His life smashed, and sorrowing in prison, he tried to comfort himself, writing these poignant but beautiful words in *De Profundis:*

> Nature, whose sweet rains fall on unjust and just alike, will have clefts in the rocks where I may hide, and secret valleys in whose silence I may weep undisturbed. She will hang the night with stars so that I may walk abroad in the darkness without stumbling, and send the wind over my footprints so that none may track me to my hurt: she will cleanse me in great waters, and with bitter herbs make me whole.

Enough of the down side but I love those passages and just had to share them. These two literary greats both went out in style, or so tradition has it. I hope Wilde's last words were as alleged—"either this wallpaper goes or I do". As for Dorothy Parker's epitaph—"pardon my dust"—I'd give a great deal to come up with something like that, but creating *bons mots* is more in Bill's line than mine, I'm afraid. "Pardon my dust" was brought to mind this week by an article in *The New York Times*. Parker left her estate to Martin Luther King Jr to be put towards the civil rights movement in America. Her ashes were interred at the headquarters of the National Association for the Advancement of Colored People but the N.A.A.C.P. is now moving from Washington DC to Baltimore. Big debate: should her ashes go with the N.A.A.C.P, or be returned to her hometown, New York City? I can imagine her amused in the middle of the argument saying "pardon my dust" once more. I hope the N.A.A.C.P. takes her with them to Baltimore. The civil rights movement was the focus of her final intentions and her gesture would heighten renewed focus on civil rights and reconciliation.

Meanwhile, speaking of birthdays—which I wasn't—today, Monday 27th July, granddaughter Jemima turns 13. Which brings to five the number of teenagers in our family. Like the others, Jemima is streaking up apace and, like her sister Olivia, mad about horses. Why, I wonder, do teenage years cause tremors in parental hearts? Actually, I don't wonder. I know. Bill and I may sometimes feel ourselves the targets of Lewis Carroll's poem ("You are old, Father William," the young man said, "And your hair has become very white.") but we're not so old that we have forgotten the joys of life with teenagers. And are perfectly happy to look on from grandparental heights and smile, especially as our children tear their hair out over the things that made us do the same years ago. And, just by the way, my hair is not white. Not as dark as it once was, and encroaching grey has blurred the Indira Gandhi streak which I loved and nurtured into place, but white it is not. My family was wont to tease me, saying my mother went white after I was born but, in this at least, I have defied genetics. Bill, on the other hand . . .

And so to dip into a new book. Pandemic difficulties continue. For some time, we have not been permitted to travel overseas without special permission but now we cannot travel south to Melbourne and the state of Victoria, and Sydney is looking a bit dicey as well. Short journeys out of town are still possible so I was amused to come across the following diary note from English novelist Fanny Burney (1752 - 1840). This week in 1791 she wrote:

> We went on no farther than to Bagshot: thirty miles was the extremity of our powers; but I bore them very tolerably, though variably. We put up at the best inn, very early, and then inquired what we could see in the town and neighbourhood. "Nothing!" was the concise answer of a staring housemaid. We determined, therefore, to prowl to the churchyard, and

read the tombstones inscriptions: but when we asked the way, the same woman, staring still more wonderingly, exclaimed, "Church! There's no church nigh here!"

Better luck with your own travels. Poor Fanny. Thirty miles is nothing to an Australian, a point we like to make to the English, no doubt to their irritation. It's a big-noting game we also like to play with Texans but that's a story for another day.

Stay well and keep safe

With love

Elaine
27 July 2020

20
Sticking Together, Like Pooh and Me

Dear Friends,

Exchange in our house this week. "Where's the plastic lemon?" Bill asks. "You know—the one we put cut lemons in." "In the fridge," I reply. "No, it's not. I've looked," complains Bill. "Look again," I say. "Try shelf above dairy shelf in door." "Oh," says Bill as he finds 'missing' plastic lemon. Dangerously egged on by the whiff of victory, I venture: "Why is it that men can never find anything? Even when it's under their noses." "Ah-ha!!" Bill counters. "If we're into gender stereotyping, why is it that women always leave the lights on?" Border skirmishes ensue.

Bill goes out to breakfast and returns having had heated agreement with fellow blokes about propensity of women to leave lights on. Existing treaty alliances, drawn up over the last several thousand years—or at least the last fifty-one of our marriage—now at risk from escalation of this conflict into something global. Please keep an eye on Belgium and Sarajevo in the next little while.

From little things big things grow. The smell of victory wafting even more strongly, I counter Bill's smug assertion (backed by distant cheering from his mates) re women and lights with the catty remark, "no wonder you couldn't find the (expletive deleted) lemon—the lights were off! SO THERE!!" Victory, I thought. *"Allons enfants de la Patrie!"* I sang heartily and we both laughed. It's an old game. Bill can't find stuff and I don't leave lights on. Well, no more than he does but neither will give in on this so we have learned to enjoy the game. That's how it is.

Which is why A.A. Milne's poem *Us Two*, which I have shamelessly misquoted above, is so fitting for Bill and me.

Wherever I am, there's always Pooh,
There's always Pooh and Me.
Whatever I do, he wants to do,
"Where are you going today?" says Pooh:
"Well, that's very odd 'cos; I was too.
Let's go together," says Pooh, says he.
"Let's go together," says Pooh.

. . . "I wasn't afraid," said Pooh, said he,
"I'm never afraid with you."
So wherever I am, there's always Pooh,
There's always Pooh and Me.
"What would I do?" I said to Pooh,
"If it wasn't for you," and Pooh said: "True,
It isn't much fun for One, but Two,
Can stick together, says Pooh, says he.
"That's how it is," says Pooh.

I grew up with A.A. Milne's poems and stories. The cadences of his poems are still in my head just as my mother read them to us when we were very young (sorry, Mr Milne!) and just as I read them to my children. I even found him useful once to start a sermon on Jacob. "King John was not a good man," Milne told us, "he had his little ways." So did Jacob. Bad ones. So do we all.

Which reminds me, I must share with you a couple of *bons mots* my friend Carol sent in response to my letter last week. Her favourite cutting remark comes from Robert, Comte de Montesquiou-Fézensac. When criticised for snubbing an acquaintance who had greeted him in the street, he apparently said, "Everyone bows to the cross. The cross does not respond". *Quelle arrogance!* Do people like Le Comte sit around thinking up lines in the hope that they'll get to use them one day? Quite possibly. It occurs to me that de Montesquiou-Fézensac would have made a good sparring partner for Oscar Wilde. They were of an age, being born in 1854 and 1855, and Wilde died in Paris. Perhaps they knew each other; age and interests suggest the possibility.

Carol's own offering from what she describes as "her younger, thinner and more cruel days", fell from her lips when a man apologised profusely for stepping on her foot at a crowded art opening. "Oh, that's all right," Carol said, no doubt smiling sweetly, "you remind me of someone I'd ignore." Umm . . . I don't think he made it to Carol's Christmas card list.

Definitely on our Christmas card list is our friend Louise, she of the ANZAC biscuits I salivated over some months ago. Louise is one of our group of singles, friends whom we've had to dinner regularly during these past pandemic months. This week we held a farewell dinner for her as, after months of complicated work and waiting, she finally received permission to travel from Australia to Denmark. Louise's partner, Minik, an internationally respected geologist from Greenland, lives in Copenhagen and coronavirus has kept them apart all year. We four and other friends spent last Christmas and New Year at Warwick's hotel in Jogjakarta. Minik returned to Denmark and Louise to Australia to spend time with her daughters. Various things prevented her leaving when she'd planned, then coronavirus and lockdown captured her in Canberra. The delay played havoc with visa arrangements and life for Louise got messily complicated.

I love the fact that the Danes have thought outside the box and introduced what translates into English as a 'sweetheart visa' for people like Louise. The days of simple single or married status only have gone. Red tape got a bit knotty here and there but Louise left on the first possible flight. As I write she and Minik will be together again. It's a lovely story for these difficult days; what began as a chance meeting at a conference in Greenland when Louise was Australia's Ambassador for Climate Change turned into a fairy-tale romance. It just proves icy poles can steam with passion. We will miss Louise greatly but will have another dinner for her when she comes back to Canberra to visit family, hopefully next time with Minik.

While on the subject of international relations (well, they come in various forms), I hinted last week at a game Australians like to play with Texans. Texas and Australia may have numbers of things in common but the one indisputable fact is size. We are both BIG. Hence a joke much favoured by Australians, including Ambassadors with appropriately friendly Australian/American audiences. In fact, I was reminded of it by Gary, who is our current Ambassador to Indonesia and admits he's used it on occasion. A visiting Texan rancher and his Australian host, an outback cattle station owner, were exchanging views on this and that, leaning casually on a stockyard fence. "Cattle! I don't call those cattle. Why, back home in Texas, my cattle are twice as big as these." Silence from Australian host. Just then a kangaroo hopped by. "What on earth's that?" asked the Texan. "Why, that's a grasshopper," came the dry reply.

Back to the subject of married relations. The Reverend J.W. Horsley, who was Chaplain at Clerkenwell Prison, wrote this month in 1886 that "a visiting wife describes her husband as a good one, and gives me as a definition, 'He doesn't get drunk *every* Saturday night'". Nor does mine so there's a mercy. However, another August reference to the married state really captured my attention. Do try to keep your eyebrows down. On August 1 in 1662 Samuel Pepys wrote in his diary:

> God forgive me, I was sorry to hear that Sir W. Pen's maid Betty was gone away yesterday, for I was in hopes to have had a bout with her before she had gone, she being very pretty. I also have a mind to my own wench, but I dare not, for fear she should prove honest and refuse and then tell my wife.

God may have forgiven him but he clearly had reason to be less certain of his wife. I can't help but notice that 1662, the date of this startling piece of self-disclosure, was also the year of the publication of THE *Book of Common Prayer.* Apparently, like many before him, and many more since, Mr Pepys kept his fingers crossed while in church.

Meanwhile 358 years later, there is much joy to be had even in shared jokes that are like comfortable old slippers. Of course, Bill does try to trip me up. "What do you think of my new glasses?" he asked the other day. I'm a bad liar and 'fessed up that I hadn't noticed. Bill shot to the high ground immediately (I would have too) but later he confessed that he'd collected them in January but had only just started wearing them! What can one do but laugh especially when he then leapt to his feet, struck a poet's pose, one hand to breast, the other elegantly thrust to the skies and wildly paraphrased Wordsworth, "My heart leaps up when I behold your eyes!" Dropping the ham pose, he added wryly that the number of organs joining in the leaping up process has declined over the years.

I declined to comment, satisfying myself with a modest blush.

Go well and keep safe,

With love,

Elaine
3 August 2020

21
Feeling Liverish!

Dear Friends,

Bill has finished restoring and painting three garden benches, almost finished a garden table, and has begun work on the four metal bird cages we brought back from Indonesia. Why we bought them is a lost memory, best attributed to a misguided urge of the moment. We're not into birds in cages. However, a small problem arose this week. Or maybe I should say fell. As Bill was busy daubing a bird cage with rust remover or summat, a flock of sulphur-crested cockatoos flew noisily overhead, screeching and squawking as is their wont, as if they're yelling "Coming through! Coming through!" He looked up and saw—splat! The results of a dive-bombing operation all over one of the newly painted benches. Desecration! He came inside to me, face set—and not to refined rapture. "We are not amused," he said in a tone of which Queen Victoria would be proud. "We are wondering whether we hate nature or not. Bastard birds! They didn't poop on that furniture till I'd cleaned it up!" I suggested moving one of those black ducks we have found deters birds from plopping on outside furniture. Why they do so is one of nature's mysteries, as why birds plop anywhere is not. Poor Bill. I was careful not to laugh until he'd returned to his bird cages. I now imagine him huddling outside in the rain, shotgun (which he doesn't have) on his knee, waiting for the criminal bird to pass.

Now here's a reader survey for you. How do you pronounce the word "poop"? Bill and I say it rhymes with "put". Our grandchildren say it rhymes with "hoop". They laugh at us and are firmly convinced we're wrong. Fun battle lines have been drawn over this word. We mutter darkly to ourselves about the influence of Hollywood etc on

Australian English and fiercely defend our pronunciation against
their laughter but they are not to be budged. Nor are we!

A piece of silliness perhaps but these are grim times for a great
many people and we could all do with a bit of humour. An article
in *The Australian* this week had the headline "Lockdown survival:
humour matters, weight gains don't". People in Melbourne are doing
it particularly tough at the moment compared to the rest of Australia.
They have a night-time curfew, renewed social lockdown with most
work and schooling home-based, mandatory mask-wearing and
increased police monitoring powers—all for six weeks, hopefully
no longer. This article says, "lockdown is horrible . . . when it gets
too much—and it will—remind yourself . . ." then lists the strictures
people in other countries have endured. Americans, Russians, British,
Spaniards, French, Indians, Brazilians and more.

Too true that there are always people worse off than whatever
we're experiencing. But for families stuck with little (any!) children in
tiny apartments or houses, desperately trying to keep up with work,
children's schooling, all the usual domestic chores *and* staying sane in
the midst of the chaos, or for the isolated, the already unemployed, the
newly unemployed faced with a reality they never dreamed would be
theirs, it's understandable they find it hard to focus on other people's
problems.

Like all human crises, the pandemic is bringing out the best in
many people but the worst in others. And such clichés do contain bits
of truth. It's the bad stuff the media tend to focus on which isn't all that
helpful for anyone. Paul Krugman wrote in *The New York Times* ten
days ago about what he calls "America's cult of selfishness" but I don't
think it would be fair to say the US has a monopoly on selfishness.
Those of you who are American are faced with horrendous problems,
both politically (I say no more!) and with the coronavirus pandemic,
and not everyone will behave well but some of us in Australia see
signs of this same 'cult of selfishness' here.

A term has cropped up about 'sovereign citizens'. "I'm a sovereign
citizen! I won't be told what to do by anyone!" In other words,
apparently, I'm above the law. The other day a video went viral (as
we all say these days; do we?) of a woman trying to enter a store
and refusing to don a mask. She yelled belligerently, "I don't have to
do that! It's my right as a live woman!" Oh really? As opposed to a
dead one? This kind of attitude doesn't give the smallest nod to the

common good. She has threatened law suits against the store, the store workers, the police, the government and so on and her lawyer says she's extremely upset by the hurtful things people are now saying about her. At least she didn't wield a knife and slash anyone's face as did a man in Brisbane. A policeman serving papers in a routine way is now recovering from serious, disfiguring wounds. The assailant was shot but is also recovering.

Krugman's article claims that the coronavirus "has revealed the power of America's cult of selfishness. And this cult is killing us". He may be right. But Australian writer Christos Tsiolkas wrote in a recent article about an overheard conversation which indicated the same thing here. On a Melbourne tram just before that city's second lockdown he heard three high school students discussing the Black Lives Matter rally they attended days before. A more than good cause to rally for but many people, including Tsiolkas, made the decision that now was not the time for that form of social protest. The common good dictated caution. Tsiolkas wrote:

> The young students were passionate about anti-racism, and they dropped the word 'privilege' a few times. But very soon their conversation turned to how COVID19 had ruined their plans for schoolies week. They had been planning to fly up to Byron Bay but that now seemed impossible. "It's so unfair," one of them sighed.

Schoolies is a getaway week many students take after final exams at the end of high school; it's mostly innocent fun but too much booze, too many drugs and too little personal discipline have led to deaths periodically.

Tsiolkas goes on to say he kept quiet. He remembers being young. Don't we all? But his mind went to the lessons of his upbringing, the things drilled into him by his hard-working immigrant parents: the gifts of patience, compassion, sacrifice and, best of all, the gift of gratitude. He writes,

> My mother crosses herself and declares, 'We're not ill and we're not homeless. Let's be thankful for that'. It was in the interplay between gratitude and the responsibilities that ensue from that understanding that my ethics and my politics were formed. That gift is my bedrock.

In all honesty, we could do a helluva lot worse, as we try to get through a horrible time and head into The Dear knows what, than think of Tsiolkas and his mother, and their wisdom, and that bedrock.

And of humour. A letter in *The Sydney Morning Herald* this past Saturday brings us back to humour. Under the heading "Those were the daze" it said:

> Remember before COVID19, when our nightly news featured murders, car crashes, corruption, political chicanery, failed relationships and drunken footy louts? Wasn't it lovely?

I guess we can all share the irony.

The fine heart of these times is shown when someone finds a way to combine compassion and humour. My friend Rebecca's mother, a theologian of some standing in her working days, is now in a retirement home. She is reasonably well but her mind wanders at times. Via Zoom, Rebecca has been reading *Winnie the Pooh* to her mother and some of her friends. Then, considering her mother's professional background, she asked if she should read from the Bible as well. "Oh, no!" her mother insisted, "people much prefer *Winnie the Pooh* to the Bible." So there we have it. *When We Were Very Young* and *Now We Are Six* rule!

Which reminds me of a snippet I have for you from The Reverend John Skinner, writing on 10 August 1823. Those of you who are preachers may sigh a little; those of you who are not, don't feel you need to emulate the huffy parishioner should you find yourself in church one day:

> I preached in the morning at Camerton a sermon, pointing out the advantages of education if properly directed, and ills arising from the neglect of it. Mrs Jarrett, I thought, did not seem much to approve of some parts of the discourse, as I now and then noticed an emphatic 'hem'. However, I am too old a soldier to be alarmed at squibs!

So there again! I have been interrupted twice while preaching by people who have fainted. It was the heat, people, not wonder at my words. The most confronting experience I've had was when a man leapt to his feet, waving a black book, presumably the Bible, and yelling, "I came to hear about Jesus! Why don't you talk about Jesus!"

"I'm getting there," I responded. Then he started heading down the aisle towards the front which focused my mind somewhat, not out of fear for myself, but because the Governor-General was present and a bunch of hunks—his Close Personal Protection Officers—was at the back of the church, weapons probably present but concealed. "Please no," I thought, "don't come any closer or this could get very, very messy." I could see the news coverage: "Attack on GG by irate parishioner foiled. In defence, assailant condemns preacher for heretical utterances". Fortunately, the man stopped and abruptly left, still waving his Bible. The coppers retreated. Who said church is never exciting?

Excitement ran hot over another dinner at our house last night. Every second Sunday now brings a delivery from the Binalong Butcher (Lamboutique: Paris, Milan, Binalong!); this week corned silverside, more of the-world's-best-sausages, and lamb's liver. Angus, Philippa and John came and, asked for their choice, they opted enthusiastically for the liver. Who knew it to be so popular? So, having just made myself a firm not-to-be-broken promise to return us to a stricter diet (remember lockdown survival, Elaine, humour matters, weight gains don't!), last night was a lost cause. Well, with liver one must have bacon, mashed potato and a rich gravy. Unconvinced that the liver would really be so popular, I cooked sausages as well. AND, given it is winter here and quinces are in season, I put some in the oven with butter and honey for hours, and hours, and hours. Oh, the aroma! Bliss!

Eat your hearts out.

Stay well and keep safe.

With love to you all

Elaine
10 August 2020

22
An Homage to Friendship

Dear Friends

And so we meet again . . . I enjoy writing each week. I think of you as I do so and the process pulls my life together comfortably. Or, rather, it is the glue of friendship which does that. Friendship and community. Communities can be close or disparate. The important thing is what gifts come from them. I heard this week about a man who many decades ago studied theology and, through a variety of strange circumstances, now finds himself with almost no commitment to a church community but writes regularly to prisoners in gaols around the country. They have all committed the same crime, one viewed generally with total abhorrence, but he has found himself reaching out to the core humanity in these individuals. His theological studies may be long behind him, and distant in almost every way from his life, but he understands his actions as a Christian imperative. He can imagine the isolation of these criminals and feels a demand to try to ease that, despite the horror of their crimes. Few of us are so strong.

Over the past weeks we've had many good times with local friends and are grateful for the gift they are to us. I've also had some happy reunions with old friends elsewhere—virtually. Who knows when we will see each other again, given travel restrictions, but that is not the main point by any means. I've heard from Jeremy, for example, who popped up in my inbox recently to my great pleasure. The times Bill and I travel to Bali each year coincide too often with Jeremy's travels to the US so it's been some years since we've been able to meet over a drink and a long chat. I wrote a while ago about Warwick and his lovely hotel outside Jogjakarta. We speak on the phone regularly. He's now been able to travel to family in Bali, and visiting another of our friends, Ross. More happy and funny phone calls.

AND I've heard again from two friends, Carl and Jo, whom we have not seen for many years. Carl was the Rector of the Episcopal Church in Mexico City and is a wonderful ebullient Texan. Jo is an expert at dealing with wonderful ebullient Texans! Carl once told us sombrely that good table manners in Texas mean keeping one foot on the floor. We four became fast friends. Carl also gave me my first practical training in parish work. I remember after a funeral he ripped the preacher's sermon apart, and shook a finger at me saying, "don't ever let me find out you've preached a sermon without mentioning the Christ!" Would I dare! Carl and his Mexican colleagues, Sergio and Carlos, who both tutored me in my first studies (both of them became bishops; Carlos is still Bishop of Mexico) gave me solid foundational training.

So many memories and stories. Just after we arrived in Mexico City, Carl came to call on me for afternoon tea in the garden. Round the corner bounded Xochitl, our inherited Great Dane. She was huge, given to bounding across the lawn like a racehorse, throwing up clumps of turf behind her. I would brace myself against a wall or whatever to try to counter her wild exuberance. Xochitl was madly over-friendly. And also seemed a bit confused as to her sexuality. Poor Xochitl. She had form. Famous for having flattened a visiting Australian Trade Minister on the dining room floor and . . . getting friendly with his leg. That afternoon she tried it on with Carl, who kept a completely straight face as I tried to haul away an animal way stronger than I and act as if all this was perfectly normal.

Talk about an ice breaker between strangers.

This incident was, however, the end of Xochitl's time with us. "That's it!" Bill declared. "F***ing the Vicar's not on!" A new home was found for her and we were all safe from her love! On the other hand, after such an incident it was all smiles and Carl and Jo became regular visitors. I remember one occasion in particular when Bill was away somewhere in the Central American part of his bailiwick. After dinner, we three went for a stroll in the garden and discovered the security guard behind the wheel of the official car, drunk, singing and with gun in hand. Not surprisingly, we didn't feel like making an issue of it. I rang the embassy so they could cope with the man.

Carl and Jo were also part of a game that grew out of one of the oddest gifts Bill received over the years of his service. Somewhere in Central America he was presented with a stuffed iguana, mounted standing upright and with a guitar in its hands. Bizarre enough but down its exposed belly was the large taxidermist's incision which had been extremely crudely sewn up. Definitely an F for fail in the art of taxidermy; ditto for any artistic form I would have thought. Bill presented the iguana to Carl and Jo as a Christmas present but one day we found it back in our house, tucked behind a pot plant. It soon became the thing we would try to sneak back to each other's houses. I've forgotten how we managed to do that but it was a fun variation on 'games people play'. We presented it to them before we left, carefully choosing a moment when no amount of ingenuity (of which they had plenty) could have returned it to us. Thanks, Carl and Jo, for good times.

Mind you, that iguana was not THE most bizarre gift Bill has been given. That honour belongs to our Indonesian time. It came during formalities at a reception we gave for young sportspeople, specifically a junior girls' basketball team from the Indonesian province of West Papua which was going on a visit to Australia. Bill was presented with a gift and, in accordance with Indonesian custom, he immediately handed it, unopened, to an officer with him. The next morning two young officers brought the package to him at the Embassy, suggesting he might like to look at it. Bill said, no, no, just enter it in the gifts register. "Ah, we think you might like to see this," they suggested. It was a carved wooden statue of a man, um, having sexual congress with a cassowary. Whoever thought that an appropriate gift for an Ambassador? For anyone! Actually, whoever thought it a good idea to produce it? We remain consumed with wonder over that gift and, no, we did not keep it. Nor do we know if it was kept as a curio at the embassy. Weird.

Given the formal restraints that commonly exist in the diplomatic world, we can probably count ourselves lucky to have received such oddities. Much more valuable, of course, have been the opportunities for friendship but there are hurdles to be faced. Communities of strangers and being a stranger among them. Facing difference in even the simplest aspects of daily life. Maintaining your own national identity in the face of such differences. Cultural clashes and shocks. Fitting oneself into other people's ways of doing things; new places, new people, new habits, new languages. This is the stuff of diplomatic life. It isn't for everyone and it demands resilience and a strong stomach. It exacts penalties, sometimes heavy, but it also rewards with a kaleidoscope of visions of human richness and ways of simply being. It has given us wonderful friendships.

It can also be hard and uncompromising. In 1971, at the end of our time in Cairo, there were many people who said eagerly, "we must meet again" and they meant it. And I said, equally eagerly, "yes we must" and I meant it too. But I looked into their eyes wondering, "will I ever see these eyes again?" and I knew I would not. Many years later, in Mexico, I met a woman with whom there was an instant rapport. We chatted happily and then the inevitable question came. What had brought me to Mexico? I wriggled in various directions but the truth had to come out. "Oh," she said. "A diplomat's wife. We can never be friends. I was friends with a diplomat's wife once and it was awful when she left. It hurt so much and I'm never doing that again." It was the last time I saw her. Yes, it does hurt, but what she hadn't realised, I guess, is what had struck me during those first years in Cairo as friends disappeared into their own futures but not mine: there cannot be the joy of friendship without the grief of loss. To cut oneself off from friendship for fear of loss is to embrace lifelessness. We aren't called to hide from life for fear of what blows we might suffer. We're called to clasp life to our breasts and dance with it. To get knocked down sometimes but to drag ourselves up and keep dancing. Sometimes in tears. Tears would be easy as I think of those whose eyes I will not see again. But we had good times together and I won't ever regret them, nor dwell on their loss.

Closer to home, each week brings nice little surprises and signs of friendship. This week, Bill's oldest friend Michael (he was best man at our wedding a thousand years ago) sent us from Sydney a packet of half a dozen face masks made by a theatrical designer who, after a wonderfully successful professional year in 2019, has had to redesign her life, so to speak, and is producing face masks. SO much nicer than the run-of-the-mill things from the pharmacy. Many thanks, Michael. I've bagged the batik one! Another reminder of an old friend . . . some days ago Bill decided to sort out 'the priest hole' in our house. It's a tiny windowless internal room which once contained, as well as wine, a large bookcase of my theology books—hence its name. Bill plays among the bottles every now and again, whistling softly to himself, arranging and rearranging. This time he turned up a bottle from 2008, the oldest he currently has, which was a gift from our friend Keith. Bill calls him "the one who got away": I met him the same night I met Bill but I married Bill! Keith and Leonie live in Adelaide. Getting there to see them seems a bit unlikely for a while but we live in hope—and the bottle will remained sealed till then.

All these things keep alive the central value of friendship. It's why I write these letters. It cements connections and pushes away the fear of loss, of you, and of travel, and wondering just when that is going to be possible again. Right now we are supposed to be in Indonesia for three weeks. Indonesia has just announced it is closing its borders to all foreigners until at least the end of this year, when it will reconsider and possibly extend the lockout.

On the other hand, I do like quiet times. Carl reminded me of a lovely phrase we learned in Mexico and has become part of our mixed-up lexicon of bits and pieces of words and expressions from various countries. *Que bonito es no hacer nada, y después de no hacer nada, descansar!* How good it is to do nothing, and after doing nothing, have a little rest!

Which Bill is not exactly doing at the moment. He has finished restoring and painting three outside benches. He's cleaned two marble ones. He has been oiling various bamboo garden screens. He appeared a moment ago saying, "I've finished all those jobs. What can I clean now?" There was a manic look in his eyes which rested just too long on me. I'm off.

Keep safe and stay well.

With love

Elaine
17 August 2020

23
Oh, What a Gift!

Dear Friends,

After last week's talk of friends and gifts, Bill and I have had fun this week thinking about gifts over the years. We rather thought we'd cornered the market in odd gifts but there are some challengers out there. Lyn wrote telling me about her husband Colin's most treasured work gift: a stuffed cane toad. Clearly, a good story came with that weird gift from colleagues because since the 1980s it has sat proudly on a shelf in his study. As Lyn says, "we dust our toad fondly".

If you don't know about cane toads your life is complete. They are ugly. Seriously ugly and seriously fecund. They are from South America and were introduced into Australia in the mid 1930s to control the sugar cane beetle. They turned out to be aggressive and adventurous explorers who have invaded large parts of northern Australia, breeding at an indecent rate and playing havoc with native species who have tried to eat them. Cane toads are extremely poisonous.

They are also one of the best reasons NOT to import species which are wont to mess with ecosystems. The *cactoblastis* moth, on the other hand, was a successful import into Australia, in this case to try to do something about the scourge of prickly pear that had taken over vast swathes of Queensland, rendering millions of acres of agricultural land useless. Various efforts had failed then, in 1912, the Prickly Pear Travelling Commission was formed. This group of scientific experts travelled the world in search of natural enemies of the prickly pear that might be suitable for Queensland. Where the cane toads were a runaway disaster, the *cactoblastis* moth was a runaway success, munching its way through, and destroying, Queensland's cactus problem. This experiment is apparently still regarded as the world's most successful example of controlling a plant pest by biological means. It has been similarly successful in other countries though it is apparently now causing trouble in North America where it's threatening native prickly pear. The best-laid plans . . .

As it happens, my maternal grandfather was a public servant in Queensland's Department of Agriculture and part of that Travelling Commission and we have the book of letters he wrote to his then fiancée, my grandmother. Perhaps typical of the times, she copied them out, carefully eliminating what she thought unsuitable for other eyes. I guess racy things like "My dear Ellen" or "your loving fiancé, Charles"! I wonder whether she knew of Isabel Burton's doing much the same thing to Sir Richard Burton's work after he died! Nevertheless, those letters are in their own way a gift from the past from grandparents I never knew.

From the personal to the public, there is a well-established world-wide system of gift-giving, most of the gifts much more mundane than the ones I mentioned a week ago. An awful lot of kitsch gets dished out and I guess much of this is disposed of as quickly and discreetly as possible. Australian public servants are not permitted to accept gifts of any great value. A cheap pen or a mug would be pushing things! There are extremes, of course. Once in Malaysia, Bill called on an extremely sophisticated, wealthy and elegant Tan Sri who presented him with a multi-coloured plastic cuckoo clock. On the other hand, in Indonesia he was given a 1982 bottle of Château Petrus. At today's price that's a drop worth $US10,379.66 ($A14,500), which amounts to a helluva lot of cheap pens and mugs. Obviously, that was declared but served (with official permission) at a dinner for the donor.

I've come in for gifts as well, but personally, not as part of any official involvement. A dear friend overheard me twittering with people discussing leather coats. I made some inane remark about not having one but if I did get one I'd want a fabulous 50s swing coat á la Audrey Hepburn in *Breakfast at Tiffany's* and in a deep imperial Roman purple. I moved on, working the room, and completely forgot what was merely a remark for a laugh. Many months later for my birthday I received a bag of purple-died baby lambskins from Turkey. So I have a purple leather coat which is fabulously eye-popping and reminds me of Cetin every time I wear it. Oh, what a gift!

And then there was a wonderful gift given me by my friend Kathryn, known to me as Flo. She called me Madge. Why we adopted these names I no longer remember but we were protective of them, turning fierce eyes on anyone who tried to use them, even our husbands, though we were a little tolerant with them. In the 1980s we were together in New York where Bill, and Flo's husband John, worked together at Australia's Mission to the UN. We introduced them to a little jewellery shop we'd discovered in Greenwich Village, a place called the Den of Antiquity which, sadly, no longer exists. For her fortieth birthday, Flo bought herself a pair of earrings there— diamond studs with pendant Texas yellow zircons. I was with her when she bought them and thought how much their simplicity and elegance suited her.

In early 1993, she gave them to me. It was at a party after I was ordained deacon and she dubbed them The Ordination Jools. It was a most extraordinary gift of love and I accepted them, grateful that this lady was part of my life. Our friendship was special to me and, I think, to her and has left me with many fond and happy memories. I wore her earrings the following year when I was ordained priest, and I wore them at her funeral in 2006. Some years ago I gave them to her daughter, Siobhan, for her fortieth birthday. It was good and right to do so. Dear Flo.

Another posting, Papua New Guinea, gave me my 'meri bangles'. These are actually the hard rubber ring seals from petrol drums which are carved with simple designs and worn *en masse*. I was given these by Yerema, the mother of two of my Papua New Guinea friends, Meg and Daisy. Yerema was a strong stately woman from Goroka in the Highlands who ruled her world with dignity and in an occasional take-no-prisoners way. I have kept my meri bangles and wear them occasionally to remind me of happy adventures in that remarkably beautiful country.

One of those adventures gave the gift of another wonderful memory. We had flown to the village of Teptep in Morobe Province where, among other things, Bill was to unveil a plaque at a sports field being named for him. (I did point out later that the plaque was new but the screws were old—just saying!) It was clearly a big thing in the area and people had walked great distances to be there when the Big Man Bilong Australia came to town. I remember looking at the mountain slopes rising high around the village and its sports field and seeing a sea of what seemed thousands of people. It was a wonderfully colourful occasion with dancing and speeches—Papua New Guineas are great orators and no speech is ever short.

Gifts were given. I don't remember what Bill was given (a penis gourd perhaps? He had a variety—for formal or casual wear!) but the moment came for a presentation to me. Two little old ladies, very small—they wouldn't have come up to my shoulder—approached, all smiles, bare-breasted and in grass skirts—*arse grass*. Between them they were holding a length of *arse grass* to wrap around me. Suddenly they stopped, there was a long pause and they began to retreat. It was more than obvious that the circumference of Big Meri Bilong Big Man Bilong Australia was way too big for their piece of *arse grass!* Another pause. I whispered out of the corner of my mouth to Bill and our daughter, Catherine, who was with us, "Either of you two laugh and you're dead meat!" The silence became deafening. Then the little old ladies appeared again, this time bearing an enormously long piece of *arse grass,* probably enough for a perimeter fence at The Sydney Cricket Ground, or maybe Shea Stadium!

Now Papua New Guineans have a great sense of humour but, in circumstances like this, with natural courtesy they wait to see how their honoured guest will react. What could I do but laugh? The joke was definitely on me and it really was funny. Once I laughed great guffaws of laughter broke out. Little children rolled around on the ground, shrieking and yelling, and it seemed as if waves of laughter swept up the mountains to the sky. I suspect this Big Meri Bilong Big Man Bilong Australia is now part of local folk lore around Teptep. There are worse fates. And, by the way, I'm not all *that* big! At least, no longer.

This talk of gifts took me to a book I've mentioned before, *Take a Spare Truss. Tips for Nineteenth Century Travellers,* published in London in 1983. The attitudes recorded in the book are stunningly politically incorrect. Here's a snippet about gifts:

> It is of the utmost importance for a traveller to be well and judiciously supplied with [presents and articles for payment]: they are his money, and without money a person can no more travel in Savagedom than in Christendom. It is a great mistake to suppose that savages will give their labour or cattle in return for anything that is bright or new: they have their real wants and their fashions as much as we have . . .

After that extraordinary piece of condescension, there are remarks about what kind and colour of beads might be acceptable (and 40 to 50 pounds weight didn't go far apparently) and the need to carry a large quantity of small change for small services. It's amazing stuff from a very different age and ends with a final suggestion that,

> . . . the traveller will probably wish to leave some token of remembrance with those from whom he has received hospitality. For this purpose a few extra pairs of pistols, knives, needles, pocket telescopes, penknives, scissors, pencils, India rubber, well bound blank books, ink-stands, toys for children and ornaments for ladies should be provided. Prints of the Queen [that's Vickie!], ministers &c., are acceptable to the British consular agents, who are generally natives.

If you have recovered from that little lot, let me assure you we've never travelled with even one pair of pistols. Nor, indeed, do we have any. I should add, however, that among the gifts Bill has received I've remembered a unique offering. In Papua New Guinea there was an enterprising man who established a business supplying poultry manure for gardens. His trucks (bright pink I think) drove round Port Moresby and bore the company name, *Mr Shit*. The owner, a Papua New Guinean whose colourful business name showed great familiarity with relaxed Australian ways, presented Bill with a company tie. The logo, a silhouette in questionable taste, was attention-getting and astonishingly frank. It is now in our son Julian's possession but I don't think it's been worn very often!

And I'm afraid Bill's career ended with one regret. He tells me he's heard it said but, no matter what outlandish outpost he visited anywhere, nobody ever said it to him: "Honoured Guest, please use my wife!"

Thank you all for the gift of your friendship in my life.

Keep well and keep safe

With love

Elaine
24 August 2020

24
A Frog He would A-Wooing Go!

Dear Friends,

I may be sorry I told you about that stuffed iguana. Last week I had the cane toad response; now Ross in Bali is trying to top both tales with a frog. Or several. Our friend Warwick, of whom I wrote some time ago, has been able to leave his hotel in Java and go to Bali and his other place, Villa d'Omah Ubud, which is also available for wonderful rental. Ross, who lives in south Bali, visited him there but was troubled by the frog chorus at night. It's 'that time of year' for frogs and they are apparently loud in their praise of mating! How to solve the problem and get some sleep?

Warwick, whom we all love to tease about it, has the same answer to any problem or need. "Mas!" he calls. *Mas* in Javanese means a man of a lower rank, in this case a member of staff. "Mas" from Warwick seems to have more tonal variations than Chinese and Japanese combined. One tone conveys the message "where are my glasses?"; another "please bring tea"; or "where are the dogs"; or, indeed, "please catch the frogs". I hasten to add that, while we tease Warwick about this "mas" call, he takes it very well. Given that he has done a huge amount for the people of Tembi, employing and training young people from many families, even paying the old people to do little jobs around about, he's earned seigneurial rank and is much respected. In Indonesia and Australia Warwick is a shared national treasure.

Back to Ubud, "Mas" and his staff team were offered an inducement: a bounty of 20,000 Rupiah for each frog they caught. They set to with alacrity. Warwick and Ross figured there'd be three or four but their projected budget was completely stuffed. Proud staff quickly appeared having captured and secured seventeen frogs. Warwick and Ross are now on the lookout for seventeen princesses who might be induced to kiss. Fun and games in Bali!

Moving on from Bali, I had an email this week from our friend Ron in Brisbane. Bill and I met Ron and Katie decades ago in Fiji and Ron wrote asking why I didn't tell any stories about our time there. Did I think it was so dull that nothing was worth recording? Well no, Ron, and you set me thinking. Ron was dean of the Anglican Cathedral in Suva and I took our children there for Sunday School. I had nothing to do with Christianity then but thought, as one did in those days, that children should know something of the religion of their culture. After a very short time, I got fed up with understanding very little, wrestling with alien bits of paper at Sunday morning services, and a mind full of questions so I tackled Ron for some answers. Thus began what I called my "yes but" sessions. Eventually, Ron suggested baptism and I baulked. "If I'm supposed to have seen the light or have had visions, then I haven't," I said defiantly. "That's fine," was his nonchalant reply. "No lights. No visions. That's fine." "Pity," I remember thinking; I was hoping for a last-minute out. A reluctant first step on the path to somewhere, in reality to ordination!

In the Anglican and Catholic traditions, baptism is followed after a year or so by confirmation. That was to be another lesson in the strange mixture of my life. On the day of the confirmation service I found myself attending a reception with Bill, dashing off to the cathedral to be confirmed, then off somewhere else for a dinner. I also found myself at the service as the only participant not dressed in white, as was the old custom. I hadn't meant to stand out in black, found the whole thing horribly embarrassing and disappeared as soon as was decently possible. Not an auspicious beginning.

For Bill and me perhaps the most important thing about Fiji is that that was where our children became 'colour blind'. When we arrived Catherine had just had her fourth birthday and Julian was two weeks shy of his sixth. They attended the Laucala Bay International School with kids from all over the world. In addition, at the cathedral children's club they were two of the less than a dozen white children. All the others were Fijian or Fiji Indian and our two learned racial equality by osmosis. Immediately obvious was that Julian and Catherine made friends by character. Julian was quickly part of a group of gorgeous kids who were bundles of mischief with huge smiles and twinkling eyes. Catherine teamed up with a group of little girls who tended to sit under a tree and discuss this and that.

Somehow, I was roped in to providing afternoon tea for the children—all sixty or more of them. One afternoon while preparing drinks in the tiny kitchen I encountered a huge spider and marched off to the dean (Ron's successor) to demand its removal. "Oh, that's just Rupert!" was the response—to which I made clear that I really didn't care what he called it, the spider went or I did. So the dean called some boys over, a group including Julian, and told them to get rid of it. I could see their faces. I could see their collective response to the task, the impish plot forming, and I headed them off to the garden away from the pews where I knew they'd planned to release my nemesis. I don't do spiders. Any kind, big or small. Part of the created order, they can do their thing but not near me.

It was in Fiji that I learned something new about Bill: he and boats are a bad mix. With another couple, Paul and Kien, we acquired the *Oilei,* which was a flat-bottomed wooden punt. It was aptly named. *Oilei* means "oops" in Fijian and lo! it came to pass. Kien flatly refused to set foot in it or allow Paul to take their daughters in it. I was not so wise. I went out once before following her example. Bill, unconvincingly, claimed his father's Royal Navy genes admirably prepared him for rum, sodomy and the lash, but, in practice, neither Bill nor I had any experience with boats so the possibility for trouble was unlimited. That single journey ended with Bill having trouble with the outboard motor (they never seem to work smoothly), getting wildly frustrated and ordering me to row. I'd never put hands to an oar and said so as I struggled with rowlocks and whatnot. The subsequent exchange went more or less thus:

Bill: "You'll have to row!"
  (I fumble)
Me: "I've never rowed before!"
Bill: "It's not that hard! Hurry up!"
Me: "I'm trying! I'm just getting the science right!"
Bill: "Row, woman, row!"
Me: "I am, for God's sake!"
  (I lose one oar which begins to disappear out to sea on the tide.)
Bill: "Don't panic!"
Me: "I'm not the one panicking!"
  (motor finally kicks in)
Bill: "Keep calm! I'll just bring the boat around and you can pick up the oar."
Me: "Pick up your own bloody oar!"

End of Farmer boating FOREVER. *Oilei* went to new owners.

That little episode of bad behaviour on both our parts aside, we enjoyed Fiji. It was a happy carefree time for the kids. They only ever wore sandals to school (a jumble of sandals lay outside every classroom); otherwise they ran barefoot, which was no problem except for the day Julian picked up the gardener's machete and dropped it on his foot. It went straight through to Mother Earth. He still bears the scar. I grabbed the kids and drove to the clinic where Bill joined us, saw the stitching-up beginning and went white, a challenge for the Black Welsh in him. Catherine refused to be separated from her bleeding brother and had to be held out of the way, so closely did she hover over the wound to watch proceedings. She must have lost that keen interest; she passed out a year or so back when her daughter Mimi had to be stitched up after a nasty accident!

Such adventures aside, Julian and Catherine had a peaceful and happy few years with lots of friends, not least of whom was 'Little Julian', son of Elizabeth, our cook-housekeeper. The three of them would climb trees and chatter together in 'Fiji English'. They had that enviable knack of children to pick up language and accents with ease, using one form of English with us and another with their friends. They also had the advantage that our garden bordered on a Fijian village. Some days they'd race in begging for money—which was when I knew the village *maramas* were making fudge.

Bill and I enjoyed our Fijian interlude. Diplomatically, it was interesting and a good place to continue to learn the foreign service game. It had its own challenges, of course. One evening we were to attend a dinner at the High Commissioner's house and dutifully arrived early to 'receive instructions'. The High Commissioner and his wife had a house guest, Lady Shaw, and I was tasked to take care of her. She was one of the *grandes dames* of the Australian foreign service, widow of Sir Patrick Shaw, a redoubtable early Australian ambassador. I privately thought Lady Shaw didn't need anyone to take care of her however . . . The challenge was to make introductions and Fijians often have very long names which pose problems for foreigners. In my anxiety, I completely fluffed introductions to Akanisi Dreunamisimisi and Sakeasi Waqanivavalagi. Fortunately, Lady Shaw was more than capable of ignoring my red-faced efforts and sailing on effortlessly.

Names in the Pacific Islands can be challenging. In those days, Australia's High Commission in Suva also dealt with a range of other inland nations including Tonga. Famously, there were dealings with one of Tonga's nobility, Baron Fukafanu'a. Officials in Canberra consistently avoided the name, always referring to "the Noble"! Fortunately, it was not an Australian politician who made one of the most egregious errors. Wanting to be courteous towards his hosts, a visiting politician said he wanted to sum up all he thought about the wonderful Fijian people and the warmth of their welcome. Unfortunately, instead of "vinaka, vinaka", ("thank, you, thank you"), he said "kanaka, kanaka". *Kanaka* was the term for South Pacific labourers (not much better than slaves) who had been taken to Australia to work on sugar cane plantations. It is a taboo word. Fijians are courteous and elegant people; they behaved as if they had not heard, but I am sure they roared with laughter afterwards in private. Maybe. I don't think that politician was aware of what he'd said; his countrymen could only blench and bang their heads on the table!

Before I finish, let me tell you of what I can only describe as an international invasion—of my dreams! Lying awake for a while last night I was wondering what I'd write to you all about today. Asleep again, I had a dream. An odd mixture of attending some conference and a cricket match. Nobody could be more uninterested in sports than I and I've not attended a cricket match since the mid 70s. We were posted in London when our friend John-of-the-shiny-shoes visited and took me off to watch an England/Australian cricket test match at Trentbridge. I watched one of Australia's great fast bowlers of the day, Dennis Lillee, race with a great loping style to bowl and managed to deliver myself of (for me) the cringe-making line, "Oh, my God, I'd hate to be on the receiving end of one of his balls!" I was an innocent. A hush fell around us, then the laughter began. Dear John began chattering, trying to ease my embarrassment. My face was as red as any cricket ball.

Back to my dream and I suddenly noticed that three American friends were playing cricket! Christopher, John David and Jeremy. Americans playing cricket and none of you from the Caribbean! All in superb cricket whites and wielding cricket bats with alacrity. I'm sorry, gentlemen, but I can't tell you how well you batted because I switched you off and went on to another dream! My apologies. I'm not sure "you're welcome to invade my dreams any time" is quite the thing to say but you certainly gave me a moment's amusement early this morning as I slogged off to the gym!

Keep safe, everyone, and do feel free to invade my dreams any time!

With love

Elaine
31 August 2020

25
A Pox on Technology!

Dear Friends,

Of course, I don't really mean that. We all know the marvels of this technological age have brought great benefits but we know equally that, when things go wrong, they go REALLY WRONG! So this week is one I could have done without. My phone died. More to the point I dropped it. People drop their phones all the time and all continues well with the world. I drop mine once. I have never dropped it before. And kaput. Clearly, it hit the floor at just that sweet spot that meant instant death. Visually, it looked no different but the right side turned out to be dead. And it was locked at the time. The thumb print shortcut would not open it. The passcode would not open it. Somewhere inside its tiny bowels it is guarding all my phone numbers. Bastard phone.

I knew immediately what this would mean. A visit to the Apple store to buy a new phone and that would almost certainly be an exercise in humiliation and exposure to some pimply youth who would speak some unintelligible computer speak which would make my mouth go dry, my face flush and my brain unable to produce a coherent sentence. As it happened, Bill was with me on this venture and I knew that wouldn't be much help. Bill uses a whale-oil-driven Nokia that is at least ten years old and, although Catherine and her family gave him an Apple SE for his birthday in June, he has found many and sundry reasons since not to make the switch to a more modern phone. Or, in fact, no reasons at all. He remains impervious to all inducements and suggestions that modern phones are SO easy. I suspect he doesn't have a reason except "just because"!

So there I was at the Apple store and the bright young man clucked a little over my phone and said, yes, that was it. Dead and unreclaimable. RIP. But, he added hastily, there's a brand new one just out and yours is SO old anyway. (I bought it in 2014!). I could choose a new one, he'd put the SIM card in, and I could then phone the Apple help line who'd tell me how I might access all my numbers. Oh, but he added, when did you last back it up? "Back it up?" I squeaked to myself. I didn't think I had to do that. I thought that was automatic. "You'll have lost everything since you last backed up," he told me and I thought maliciously, "don't sound so satisfied!"

This was not going well. Trying to maintain a modicum of dignity, I bought a phone and the two of us slunk out of the shop, I hoping not fall over my feet, which seem to go wobbly when I get nervous. We held our heads as high as we could, muttering to ourselves about the conversation among Apple staff at drinks after work. "OMG, you've no idea what I had to deal with today. This old couple who had no idea about anything. She didn't even know about backing up her phone!"

Actually, I did but I'll get to that. The thought of dealing with the Apple help desk was enough to make me blench but the one good thing in my life about mishaps with technology is SUPERBEN. Ben is a wonderful young man, a computer engineer and incredibly tolerant of plaintive ties of "Ben! Help!" when something goes wrong or needs to be installed. Ben came and set the phone up though I still do not have my contacts sorted. Despite a helluva muddle over passwords and answers to security questions (how could I possibly remember what answers we'd given to questions we had forgotten we'd been asked?), we got there. Now I have all those questions and answers carefully recorded against some future disaster. Ben came again for round two of *Operation Resurrection* after which life-as-we-know-it can resume. He also restored self-confidence and dignity for me by telling me I was right: back-up is automatic because that's the way he has set up our system. Wonderful man. All of us need a SUPERBEN in our lives, especially if the first flush of youth disappeared before things like computers and mobile phones arrived to plague us. We've told him he can never leave Canberra. He smiles and reminds us that that's what his parents say too. They happen to be great friends of ours so I think we can corral him on both flanks.

By way of soothing respite from technological problems, spring has sprung, blossoms are out, and the weather is mild if still a bit fresh. All the roses have been pruned and new plants have gone in where needed. Ben's parents, Sarah and Ian, are coming round in a day or two for a companionable session of thinning, digging up and planting out, particularly of hellabores which are astonishingly fecund plants, and chopping up clumps of potted orchids. After our labours we'll idle over a rewarding gin-and-tonic and lunch and enjoy gorgeous spring weather. Ian and Sarah are both Anglican priests (actually Sarah is a bishop—the first woman to be elected to a diocese in Australia) and great gardeners. I'm delighted to have them for a day, not only for gardening and friendship, but to be able to give excess plants away to a happy home.

This weekend it was time to pour quantities of diluted worm wee from Ada's worm farm around the garden, a task accompanied by a litany of remarks to the plants about doing the right thing by us and growing or I will rip them out by the roots! Do threats work with plants? Piles of compost will be spread as well which reminds me of someone from our Fiji days. A doctor and a priest, George Hemming, who would declare stoutly: "there are two things in life I believe in— the Church of England and compost!"

George ran the Bayly Clinic, a welfare centre where I worked as a volunteer, together with his support professionals, among them the remarkable Sister Betty Slader. She terrorised all of us working at the Clinic but for 'her people' she was nurse, midwife, shepherd of orphans and teacher of faith. Betty drove anywhere, forded rivers, walked mountains. Wherever people needed her help, Betty went. She kept a supply of coffins under beds in her home; she found she always had need of coffins for families too poor to buy one to honour their dead. She founded the St Christopher's Children's Home in Suva and years after I knew her she became the first woman ordained priest in the Anglican Diocese of Polynesia. I remember Sundays at the Anglican Cathedral in Suva when Betty would arrive in her van with another load of people, adults and children, to be baptised. 'Rice baptisms' we thought them, there were so many, but we were probably being unfair.

Betty was an icon of goodness even if a bit of a bully. She was tough on most people but especially, I think, those she thought were the well-fed rich enjoying life's consolations. I knew she meant me and I was terrified of her. We became friends in the end and now and again she'd call by our house for a whisky at the end of the day. People like

Betty are a bit shaming to those of us who aren't like her because such gutsiness is packaged with love. Gruff, tough, and plainspoken but love nevertheless. I admired her, and I admire those like her, hugely, because I know I wouldn't be much good at what they do so well.

We volunteers would gather at the Bayly Clinic early each weekday morning to prepare rations of rice, flour, milk powder, tinned fish, and milk biscuits for the children, and these would be distributed to our clients. One of my jobs was to handle the ration cards each family presented, a task which eventually gave me scabies. I've never known such an awful itch and it was a salutary experience seeing tiny babies covered with scabies. It was easily treated by a cream which our people couldn't afford. We provided it. We could afford it. Working at the Clinic exposed us to a different and confronting world. I remember women and girls scarred and cowed by wounds, sometimes inflicted by husbands, sometimes by controlling mothers-in-law. The most horrifying damage was often caused by kerosene burns.

The Bayly Clinic was the only place in the late 80s where these brutalised women could go for help and I found myself challenged, repelled, angry, and deeply troubled by what I saw, as well deeply grateful that my life was so different. I remember also an ethical question the Clinic faced as it provided the women with contraceptives, specifically a form which was banned around that time in Australia because of its detrimental side effects for some. The women begged for this Depo Provera contraceptive. They were desperate not to have any more babies, and especially not girls. We were regularly asked to take their daughters as they grew old enough to attract attention from the men in their families, from male relatives and family friends.

Should the Clinic have provided these women with the one thing that might have eased their lives, even if there was a risk to their health? The mothers begged us, for themselves and for their daughters as the only way to try to protect the girls from lives like their own. Hearing these stories, looking into eyes pleading from scarred and burned faces, was a daily challenge for us all at the clinic. A minute challenge in comparison with the challenge their lives were for them. I carry some of those faces in my mind still. And I am still not sure of the right answer to my own question about whether that contraceptive should have been given.

On a lighter note, when I wasn't gardening this week I was reading or writing—or trying to write—and happened across a 1920 comment from Virginia Woolf which is a comforting reminder that the literary greats don't just churn out their works. She felt listless, she said, after two months of writing fiction, adding that she began to wonder

> what it is that I am doing: I suspect . . . that I have not thought my plan out plainly enough—so to dwindle, niggle, hesitate—which means one's lost . . . An odd thing the human mind! So infinitely shying at shadows.

Ah, procrastination! Such a comfort to know one is not alone!

Finally, I have to tell you that tales of amphibians are still trickling in. Lyn has written to say that she and Colin were walking around the Hebridean Isle of Islay one day and stopped to chat to a elderly Scot who was sitting in the sun, outside his old, very Scottish home, admiring his view over the Loch. They remarked about how lovely it must be to be able to watch seals romping in the Loch every day. The old man erupted with bad grace: "The Government won't give me permission to shoot them! They honk and bonk all night long . . . You try sleeping with that!" I think that would be the moment to retreat in haste.

With that, it's time to set my capricious, faithless, and niggling mind to another job. As I tidied my desk yesterday, I'll have to resist some other piece of procrastination!

Perhaps I'll go and pick some violets.

Keep well and keep safe

With love

Elaine
7 September 2020

26

To Me, Fair Friend, You Never Can Be Old

Dear Friends,

This week I am in pensive mood. Never far from my mind in past days has been Vera, whom I only met perhaps twice, who died last week. Vera was married to DeWitt, one of the most influential people in my life. He and Vera were both widowed some time before they married and they enjoyed many happy years together; now he grieves deeply and I grieve for him in his loneliness.

Though I have not seen DeWitt and Vera for many years, they are nevertheless part of the reason I write to you all each week. The community of friendship is no small thing and, especially in these days when we cannot travel, when liberty is hedged around with this and that prohibition, friendship needs to be expressed and enjoyed in every way possible. Just after I learned of Vera's death, I was driving somewhere thinking of DeWitt, and of you all, and I had to blink away tears. A parade of faces passed through my mind, of the many people I have called "friend" in all kinds of places over the years and who are now gone from my life. I see their eyes and their smiles. I've said before that I will not regret those lost friends for we had good times together but that does not mean I cannot grieve their loss now and then.

This particular story goes back to the 1980s when Bill and I were in New York. We attended a church, All Saints' E60th Street, popularly called All Saints' Bloomingdales because it was half a block from that great store. It was also directly across the street from Serendipity, where we often took the kids for lunch after church. On one memorable occasion, Julian devoured what was advertised as "the world's biggest hamburger", followed by the world's biggest ice-

131

cream sundae. It looked like a litre of ice-cream topped with oceans of cream and toppings. My stomach shrivelled at the thought of the consumption but I had already learned that growing boys are a whole other and very special breed!

De was the rector of All Saints' and had been for many years. I was an ignorant new Christian in those days, with no idea how lucky I was to be learning about the Christian faith, church and liturgy at All Saints'. It was home to a wonderful professional choir, its liturgies were honed and beautiful and they taught me something of the mystery of God, of encountering the Holy. All Saints' E60th offered the very best of Anglo-Catholic worship: reverent, sincere and unfussy.

Just before we left New York for Mexico, De took me to lunch and, over white wine, said "so when are you going to be ordained?" I nearly fell into my wine glass. Everyone knew this man's reputation. He was 'a king-maker', his opinion much sought in church affairs, but also a public opponent of the ordination of women. Measured, not strident, a reasoned thinker, a godly man, a leading figure in the temperate middle among opponents, but an opponent nevertheless. This was not a man to make light of such matters but there was no question about the seriousness of his words; I could see that in his eyes. I discovered later that De wrote to the appropriate authorities in Canberra telling them of his personal views but recommending me for ordination. I was delighted that De later changed his position on the ordination of women to the Anglican priesthood.

I have not been back to All Saints' for many years but that parish, with De as Rector and Chip as curate, remains a vivid memory. It was there I began liturgical service. And it was later, when Chip was Rector of Christ Church New Haven in Connecticut that, during periodic visits, I received more invaluable liturgical training. I would arrive and be given a roster for the duration of my visit; it was tough and little quarter was given but I, like the seminarians from Yale Divinity School who were assigned there—friends like Susan, Carol and Stephen (who later became Rector of Christ Church)—received excellent training.

And here we are! My journey to priesthood, and ministry since, all began with De's question and a glass of wine in the Irish Pub down the street from All Saints'. At least his question brought into focus what had been brewing away under the surface. I am grateful to De for his teaching during my three and a half years in his parish, for taking the trouble to talk and make me think, and for supporting me against his own convictions at that time.

These sorts of memories are all part of the business of community and friendship of which you are all members. Another memory also floated to the surface this week. Of that 2007 Garuda plane crash in Jogjakarta. It was an awful time but one particular matter became really important. During the weeks and months after the crash, people had one question for me: what do we do with the business cards of our friends who have died? How do we throw them away and delete their names from our phones? I said you do it liturgically. You need ritual.

For two friends, Ruth and Rowley, this led to a ceremony on the beach at the Conrad Hotel in Bali. I asked hotel staff for a large woven and beaded Bali gift basket with a lid, and a lot of white frangipani blossom. Rowley had a bottle of champagne given him by Liz just before she'd died in the crash so I suggested he bring that. The hotel staff provided champagne glasses and also arranged for some local Balinese sailors to bring a boat. On a bright Bali morning, we gathered on the beach. I'd written some short prayers, we put the cards among the blossoms in the basket, lit the cards, then poured champagne on the ashes. A quick sip of champagne toasting Liz and our other dead colleagues, and we clambered into the boat to be taken out beyond the reef and the waves. There, with a final prayer, I placed the basket in the calm waters of the sea; Liz's spirit was returned to the Creator God.

Of course, back on shore we finished the champagne and took ourselves off for a celebratory lunch. Liz, gregarious soul, would have enjoyed that. There were a couple of interesting sidelines to that morning's ceremony. We were amused at being photographed by Japanese visitors for whom we were some kind of tourist attraction. More importantly, we realised that we had inadvertently displayed for the Balinese something they had not seen and could not imagine: westerners engaged in a spiritual exercise. Spirituality and liturgical expression are part of daily life in Bali. All Balinese participate in regular ceremonies and processions, as well as making offerings at the shrines that are tended in every home and store. Such ritual is not part of a 'Bali Theme Park'. It is as automatic as tea or coffee in the morning. Respectful, therefore, of what they were witnessing, the hotel staff and various other people watched our ritual with great courtesy. The boatmen refused to accept payment for their services.

Now this week as I trawled through my computer contact file (I'm still discovering gaps after that phone disaster) I came across names of friends who have died. There were long moments of remembering tinged with sadness and words from Dylan Thomas pushed their way forward: "do not go gentle into the night . . . rage, rage against the dying of the light!" But they are gone and I knew it was time to let them go. I prayed for each of them as I deleted their names, gone from my computer but not from my mind. Thomas's evocative words hold so much of what we feel as we grieve but I have also recalled this week other fine words about facing the disappointments and the grief that assail us. Elegant, full of hope, wisdom and inspiration, they are the concluding words of the autobiography of British diplomat and historian Duff Cooper (Viscount Norwich) and speak eloquently of what it is to face broken dreams from the past, unresolved dreams in the present, and the mystery of the future:

> Life has been good to me and I am grateful. My delight in it is as keen as ever and I will thankfully accept as many more years as may be granted. But I am fond of change and have welcomed it even when uncertain whether it would be for the better; so, although I am very glad to be where I am, I shall not be too distressed when the summons comes to go away. Autumn has always been my favourite season, and evening has been for me the pleasantest time of day. I love the sunlight but I cannot fear the coming of the dark.

It has been a quiet week of sadness and remembering. In addition, yesterday I preached at my local church for the first time in seven months—on forgiveness. Next week I will preach again—on grace. Looking out from the pulpit yesterday, I was reminded by joy of the importance of you all, of community, as during so many of the previous days I had been reminded of the same things by grief. I prayed for you all during that service, for Vera, for DeWitt in his new loneliness, for Liz and for my other lost friends. And today I add to my prayers my friend Christopher, freshly thrust into grief for his friend, Marvin, who has just been diagnosed with cancer.

The grace of God be with you all. Perhaps as we each think of friends, whether with joy or with sorrow, we can borrow from Shakespeare saying, "to me, fair friend, you never can be old".

Take care and keep safe

With love

Elaine
14 September 2020

27
Has Anybody Seen My Mouse?

Dear Friends,

So who left an outside door open? Neither of us is 'fessing up. Deep innocence stamped upon both our faces, we have settled for something like "that'll teach us to get carried away with the lovely mild spring days and leave doors open"!

Oh well, at least it's only a mouse and not the baby python Catherine had to wrangle in her kitchen some months back. And it's put me in mind of A.A. Milne's poem from my childhood:

> Has anybody seen my mouse?
>
> I opened his box for half a minute,
> Just to make sure he was really in it,
> And while I was looking, he jumped outside!
> I tried to catch him, I tried, I tried . . .
> I think he's somewhere about the house.
> Has anyone seen my mouse?
>
> Uncle John, have you seen my mouse?
>
> Just a small sort of mouse, a dear little brown one,
> He came from the country, he wasn't a town one,
> So he'll feel all lonely in a London street;
> Why, what could he possibly find to eat?
> He must be somewhere. I'll ask Aunt Rose:
> Have you seen a mouse with a woffelly nose?
> He's just got out . . .
>
> Hasn't anybody seen my mouse?

Nonetheless, with respect to Mr Milne and his wit, we don't plan on harbouring any mice so Bill headed to the hardware store. "I'm off to buy a feeding trough for Mickey," he said, the glint of murder clouding his eyes. I suggested more than one trap given the unwanted guest got a pretty free run of the place barring the west wing, to which the door will remain firmly closed. We call it the West Wing, not because of any political ambitions, or because we rather fancied the TV series, but because it is actually a wing on the west side of the house. By the way, I'm not scared of mice. Now, if it were a spider in my bedroom, or my study, I'd have packed my bags and gone in a trice! Spiders and I are not a happy mix, or only momentarily until death us do part! Splat!

When we bought this house in 2004 we had to be extremely careful to keep outside doors closed. The previous owners were cat people and their cat (an enormous bundle of white fluff with mean little eyes—how could they love it?) ran the local cat club. The laundry and kitchen doors also have cat access things which were apparently always left open so any neighbourhood cats could come and go as they pleased. Those cat doors were firmly closed as soon as we moved in and have remained so. At first we had a parade of yowling cats outside demanding entry. I don't remember what eventually deterred them. Possibly a hose sprayed around carelessly? I'm not anti-cat but if I want one, I'll get one; I'm not partial to whingeing and whining from other people's animals. And that also goes for Dash, a neighbour's Dachshund which goes ballistic when we go near our adjoining fence. Dash may have received the water spray treatment. Possibly. When we are away, Ada keeps an eye on the place and has spoken of Dash in hate-filled tones. What she has got up to . . .

The animals that give most people trouble here are the possums. They're native animals so one is not permitted to harm them in any way, let alone kill them. They invade gardens at night and are particularly partial to fresh tips, like rosebuds or new shoots of vegetables and herbs. Not content with infuriating keen gardeners with this night time foraging, possums get into house roofs, making nice dry nests for their babies then spending the nights running rave parties over the ceilings. I gather the fine for killing possums is pretty hefty but people do manage to catch them then drive way out of town to leave them in exile far from friends and family.

Unfortunately, possums are territorial and fond of their own stamping grounds so they'll return if they're not taken a long way away. Nobody admits to doing this, of course, because one is expected to tolerate the dear little things and call the official possum-catchers who might agree to remove them. The trick to success, I'm told, is to take them over water. Angus tells a funny story from his childhood of his uncle's catching possums and, under cover of deep darkness, rowing across the lake near their house to leave the captured animals on the other side. The only trouble was that a friend was accustomed to row in the opposite direction on the same mission! The possums doubtless enjoyed this free taxi service.

For completely unknown reasons, the possums don't misbehave in our garden. I see them at night making like trapeze artists on the telephone lines along our back fence. I've seen their droppings on the paths. But they leave my plants alone. I've not come across a single nibbled rosebud. No fresh herbs have been chewed. We seem to have well-behaved possums around though perhaps it's just that the neighbours' plants are more lush and tasty than mine. I'm happy not to be in competition with them and am keeping very, very quiet about it.

It has to be said that most (all?) Australians think the New Zealanders have the right idea about possums. Some stowed away and ran to freedom in New Zealand where they have been breeding like rabbits at an outrageous rate (the possums, not the New Zealanders). It's open season on possums there and they have virtue on their side: the possums count as feral non-natives (being Australian!) and native animals must be protected from them. With typical New Zealand ingenuity they have created a vibrant industry using possum fur. I particularly love my NZ possum fur socks during Canberra's winters and they were my saving grace one year when we visited our friend Chip in the wintry depths of Quebec.

Speaking of wildlife, the ongoing saga of divesting ourselves of books unearthed something we'd both forgotten, a book of alleged wit and wisdom from 1984 called *The Whingeing Pom's Guide to Australia*. We're going to have fun with this book over the next weeks!

In case any of you is unaware, Australians call the English "Poms". Derivation is disputed. Some people think the term has something to do with pomegranates and have pointed out that D. H. Lawrence, in his 1923 novel, *The Kangaroo*, which was set in Australia, wrote that

"Pommy is supposed to be short for pomegranate. Pomegranate ... is [a] near enough rhyme to immigrant ... Furthermore, immigrants are known in their first months before their blood 'thins down', by their round and ruddy cheeks". Be all that as it may, Australians have long made fun of the British as whingers, complaining about the weather, the French and us. Poms reciprocate in a variety of ways and there is much fun all round as we colonials do battle with the ould enemy.

In this vein, the dust jacket to *The Whingeing Pom's Guide* makes the following claim:

> Australia is thousands of miles from civilisation and one of the last untamed frontiers. Outside the urban areas a seething mass of sinister, predatory wildlife falls over itself in the attempt to fill you with deadly poisons . . . This book will persuade you to stay in your hotel throughout your stay.

The author then writes sections like "It Just Jumped Out at Me!", "Identifying the Species" and "The Keep Moving Guide". Australian readers would snort with derision at this attempt at humour and suggest Pommie readers take the advice of the last of these sections and leave quickly but, all the same, we get far too much pleasure out of the teasing game!

Tucked into the book we found a forgotten treasure. A handwritten letter to Bill, on British Embassy notepaper and dated 11 May 1989, which draws his attention to a piece in *The Economist* allegedly quoting *The Lonely Planet Guide to Australia* and saying "One in three Australians works for the government, one in ten is unemployed. At times it is difficult to tell which is which".

The book is, of course, spectacularly politically incorrect. It says all the things one cannot, and ought not, say, and promotes the idea of an empty land up for grabs. Here's a bit from the opening page:

> Probably the most remarkable thing about Australia is the number of times it has been discovered. [Really? Tell that to our First Australians!] From as early as the 13th century the Chinese, Malays, French, Spanish, Portuguese and Dutch all appear to have run into a 'great southern continent'. But although half the world kept bumping into the place, it is perhaps significant that no-one actually laid claim to it until America was no longer available as a penal

colony, when convicts were shipped to Australia. These were known as Insisted Passages. Using forced labour, the British Government planned to make their continental penitentiary secure by constructing a vast wall around the entire coast line, but as a cost-cutting measure the Government filled the sea with sharks instead.

Please nobody give Mr Trump this reference or he might claim historical precedent for his plans for the US/Mexican border.

And, non-Australians, please don't take all this seriously. Do not be afeared of deadly wildlife in Australia. We live our lives here in considerable comfort, rarely encountering the more deadly things like red-back, funnel web and trapdoor spiders, crocodiles, box jellyfish, taipans, adders, vipers and sundry other snakes, and Great White Sharks. Even emus, who look as bad-tempered as camels, won't do you in even though one did once draw blood from one of my fingers as I was handing a child a peanut butter sandwich at a picnic. Who knew emus are partial to peanut butter?

As a last titbit for this week, here's the amusing introduction to the *The Whingeing Pom's Guide's* chapter "Oh well, back to the drawing board":

> On the sixth day God filled the world with all manner of living things, starting at the top and working downwards. The creative process is always fairly tiring and a project as large as this could only have been shattering. It is, therefore, hardly surprising that by the time He got around to doing Australia, His concentration was beginning to slip. When He created the kangaroo He felt somewhat apprehensive; when He produced the platypus He knew it was time to call it a day.

Amen, and again we say Amen!!

Moving on, Bill's just told me that yesterday he deliberately left an outside door open to tempt the mouse to escape. As noted above, he's taken to calling it Mickey. Why not Minnie, I want to know, but it is of no moment; I'm impartial when it comes to killing mice. As Mickey/Minnie has not been seen since, and as Bill's traps with tempting cheese have been spurned, we can only assume the mouse sniffed death from one direction and freedom in the other and made the sensible choice, retreating to our garden or someone else's.

Speaking of death, Bill has confessed to me just now that our dinner for six people tomorrow evening is actually for eight. He forgot to count us. He will live, if only because I always over-cater. I'd rather live on leftovers than not have quite enough. That looks *pinche* as we learned to say in Mexico. Mean and miserly. That being said, Bill gets the last laugh. His email inviting Angus said ". . . we are having roast pork from Binalong. Interested? If I know you, you will reply before the oink is dry".

Oh dear.

Keep well and keep safe

With love

Elaine
21 September 2020

28
Valete Heroes!

Dear Friends,

Clio's blue-tongued lizards have woken from their winter hibernation and are feeding. This, it would seem, is up there with blossoms and wild daisies as a sign that spring has really sprung. Like her whole family, Clio is animal-mad but she tends to charmingly eccentric choices in her pets. Her cousins, Olivia and Jemima, tend more to dogs, cats and guinea pigs and are horse-mad which is a bit more usual and comes with its own issues, of course, but horses are physically beautiful animals. Lizards don't quite fit that description! Nor do Clio's last pets, her stick insects. No-one knew whether these were male or female, or a mixture. They grew and grew then some or all of them bred. At last count before a new home was found for the tribe there were 347 eggs. I don't think Catherine and Garth had too much trouble convincing Clio that a major management problem had arisen and relocation to the bush was the best solution.

I wasn't sorry to see them go; I found their defensive ploy of rocking back and forth oddly distasteful and their plump naked bodies repellent. Weird creatures. But Clio loved them. One amusing memory about the stick insects was the the sight of our friend Ada's face when Clio presented her with a present, a little bag tied with silk ribbon. Face set to innocent seriousness Clio, told Ada, "This is for your undies drawer. It smells like eucalyptus and that's because it's dried stick insect poo and they only eat eucalyptus". We all sucked in our cheeks and avoided each other's eyes. I've never asked Ada what she did with the gift.

Undeterred by their departure, Clio began immediately saving pocket money to buy the pair of lizards. Clio apparently comes from the same stable as the young sister of my friend Christopher. She would bring home what she thought was a waif or injured or stray animal. Like the possum found by the roadside. And the large snapping turtle minding its own business but hauled off to be a domestic pet. Apparently the child was convinced to restore its freedom after it snapped a pencil in two. Meanwhile, back in our house, not a sign has been seen, nor a squeak heard, from our invading mouse. We think Mickey/Minnie did make a successful break for freedom.

Canberra is bursting with blossom. September's Floriade festival isn't on this year because of the pandemic and social distancing rules still in place. It's very popular and brings big crowds of tourists and tourist dollars to the capital each year. In lieu of a single venue, the festival gardeners have spread throughout the city planting small gardens in all kinds of places. Over a million bulbs have gone in as well as a large range of other flowers. Canberra is looking pretty in a rainbow of colours.

Which is just as well as spirits need brightening in these election times. You may well think that the US election is the main game at the moment but here in The People's Democratic Socialist Environmentally-Sustainable Republic of Canberra election fever is high and roadsides are bristling with party political banners and boards. I am so not interested that I have to keep checking the date of the election. The Australian Capital Territory has a population of 429,834 as against Washington DC's 705,749 (thank you, Prof. Google) which makes me wonder why here in Canberra we have the full catastrophe of a government with cabinet, ministers, an ever-burgeoning budget and taxes and lots of self-important pomposity (as opposed to ditto at the federal level). Thirty-odd years ago we voted against establishing this Territory government, preferring a simple civic council, but it was foisted upon us anyway. Objecting makes me sound old, so enough.

I'm much more interested in two women who served their nations and have just died—Ruth Bader Ginsburg in America and Susan Ryan in Australia.

With RBG, as everyone seems to be calling her, it's become a cliché to wonder that so much could have been achieved by so tiny a woman. But it's true nonetheless and why should it matter that she was a wee thing? That woman's brain was bigger than most people's. I have been moved to tears reading about her and watching her casket being taken ceremoniously from the Capitol. (The first woman to lie in state in the Capitol! Why no woman before?) Nearly all her former clerks lined up on the marble steps of the Supreme Court; female members of Congress, Republican and Democrat, stood on the steps of the Capitol—all paying their respects to this giant of a woman. There could not have been a better tribute written about her than that published in *The New York Times* by Afro-American Republican Eric L. Motley who was Special Assistant to George W. Bush: 'My Unlikely Friendship With Ruth Bader Ginsburg'. What emerges from this and so many other tributes is what a seriously nice person she was; a statement also true of her husband Marty. How good for Motley and all those other young lawyers to have been mentored and befriended by this couple.

Susan Ryan I met many years ago when we first went to New York. Bill was assigned temporarily to the Australian Mission to the UN for the September to December deliberations of the General Assembly. Susan Ryan's former husband was posted to the Mission. My memory of her is of a strong woman (in a brown dress!—why should I remember that!), one with whom I felt small. She became a Labor Party politician, was the first woman to serve in a Labor federal cabinet, as Minister for Education and Youth Affairs and later as Minister Assisting the Prime Minister for the Status of Women, and was the architect of the Sex Discrimination Act of 1984. After leaving parliament in 1988 she was heavily involved in, amongst other things, the movement for Australia to become a republic. She became the inaugural Age Discrimination Commissioner in 2011 and Disability Discrimination Commissioner in 2014.

Their struggles for equality for all people, and rights for women in particular, have sent my mind scurrying through the years remembering experiences I have had of bullies and bastards, of how easy it is to be intimidated, and how draining the efforts to resist their bad behaviour. I had reason recently to recall a group of young Anglican seminarians (not in Australia) for whom I had done a lot of work and who, when they found out its female authorship, took my papers and publicly and ritualistically burned them. A deliberate insult, utterly lacking in grace and quite contrary to the gospel of Christ. Then there was the priest who hissed and whispered at me,

"If you were a proper priest, you wouldn't have any trouble with your legs!" There's something horrible about being hissed at. This too was graceless; it was also malicious and dripping with spite. He became a very senior cleric. One should never make the mistake of forgetting that the Church is a human institution and, like all institutions, full of good but blotched and stained by the bad.

Valete Ruth Bader Ginsburg and Susan Ryan. We owe them so much. And we can only try to emulate their bravery and hard work to make life better for all people. It is my hope and prayer that young women today don't face what my generation faced. They have been brought up in a different world with different mores so perhaps they will be stronger, and there are now more men who realise that bullying and bastardry are simply wrong.

On a lighter but related note, there are ways and ways of being influential. I was amused and had to laugh at myself over one instance. A conference for ordained Anglican women was held in Canberra some years back and the then Governor-General, Dame Quentin Bryce (a seriously successful lawyer) invited delegates to Government House for afternoon tea. Later a group of the young women told me how they had agonised over what to wear. I said that they would always be correctly dressed anywhere in clerical dress. Ah, they said, but we remembered a time when you said one is always well-dressed in pearls. So they had all gone out and bought pearl necklaces to wear to the G-G's tea! God knows when I made that rather fatuous remark but the dear things had remembered. By the way, I stand by my words.

I was reminded this weekend of another loss to our world: Clive James, Australian poet, critic, essayist and broadcaster, who died last year. Just before his death he completed one last book, an anthology of his favourite poems, accompanied by commentary, critique and personal anecdotes. *The Fire of Joy: Roughly Eighty Poems to Get by Heart and Say Aloud* it's called and is being published by Pan Macmillan. "The poems I remember," he wrote, "are the milestones marking the journey of my life." (Exactly as Anne Fadiman, of whom I wrote some months back, wrote: "Books wrote our life story . . . they became chapters in it themselves".) James moved to Britain in 1962, one of that group of brilliant young Australians including Germaine Greer and Robert Hughes who left for what was then seen as a bigger field. James was a huge intellect and an outstanding writer but also a larrikin. Always known as "The Kid from Kogarah" he delighted us with his wit as well as his poetry. And the *chutzpah* from his time as a TV host when he joined Luciano Pavarotti to welcome in the New Year singing Auld Lang Syne! Now that's bold!

Although James didn't return to Australia and mourned that, in the end, illness would prevent one last return, he didn't regret his choice to leave; neither did he cease to love his homeland. "When I myself come back it will be in a box of ashes, but I chose the right spot to be born, just as I chose the right profession—poetry—and followed it to the end." This is what he wrote about Australia's landscape as an inspiration for great poets:

> Australia spreads out indefinitely while only rarely piling up, and even then it seldom piles high: occasionally there are a few bumps the size of the Cotswolds, but never even a single Himalaya. From space, which begins at low altitude, there is not much down there except rock, with stretches of scrub for variety. At the edges there is some green country, but it soon runs into the surf. More often than not it is hot and bright enough to burn your skin. The whole layout looks as if it were dreamed up by Dorothea Mackellar—'I love a sunburnt country'—except she makes it too exciting. The place is huge: as big as America. But you have to search hard to find anything going on. There is a terrific urge to get not much done.

That is rather typical of James's laconic style. He does irony beautifully. He dedicates this last book to the next generation, urging them to take up writing and reading poetry. "Get on your feet and declaim!" he urges. I may not be a poet but the preacher in me says "amen!" to that. Preachers will never be worth diddlysquat until they learn to write for the ear, play with words, and squeeze every ounce of meaning from them. Gently.

In one vital respect, Clive James has great contemporary currency. It seems these days that reasoned argument has gone out of fashion. Belligerence, aggressive silencing, de-platforming and extreme condemnation have become tools of trade both within academe and without. "Agree with my opinion or we will run you out of town, shame you and deny you a voice" seems a modern mantra across left and right. So much for freedom of speech. It all brings to mind a furious controversy in the 1960s between opposing groups of English literature academics at Sydney University: those who followed Professor Leavis

and his preferred "great literature" and those who didn't. James (an
anti-Leavisite) wrote of what he described as "the Leavisite brand of
odium theologicum [which] had all the characteristics of totalitarian
argument, right down to the special hatred reserved for heretics". He
went on:

> Of all the moral lessons [Leavis] had to teach, the one that
> stuck was the one he taught inadvertently . . . he labelled
> his literary opponents so scandalously that when he tried to
> condemn Stalin he had no harsh words left over. If he had been
> asked to give his opinion of Hitler and Himmler, he would not
> have been able to summon up any terms of disapprobation
> that he had not already lavished on [others] . . . He had given
> up his sense of reality . . . He was a self-saboteur.

Vale Clive James. I'm buying his last book as an early Christmas
present for myself so I can settle down and learn of the poet's art
from the words of a master. Bill and I are still to tackle his renowned
translation of Dante's *The Divine Comedy*. It's slipped down in the
pile of 'must reads' and needs to be returned to the top. Then we
can stop feeling intimidated by our friend Keith who has read it *and*
Longfellow's translation as well!

But I've just had another gift. This past Saturday was the feast
day of Bishop Lancelot Andrewes (1555-1626), who managed to
survive three monarchs (Elizabeth I, Mary Tudor and James I)
during those turbulent and frequently dangerous religious times. He
is to be remembered with reverence as one of the translators of the
Authorised Version of the Bible, aka *The King James Version*. Ada come
round on Saturday morning to give me a bottle of Laphroaig single
malt whisky (my favourite) in honour of the great man. Andrewes
was much revered, as demonstrated by lines (modernised I think)
from *Upon Bishop Andrewes' Picture before his Sermons*, a poem by
Richard Crashaw (1613-1649):

> This reverend shadow cast that setting sun,
> Whose glorious course through our horizon run,
> Left the dim face of this dull hemisphere,
> All one great eye, all drown'd in one great teare.

Vale Bishop Andrews. As soon as my book arrives I shall pour myself a dram or two of Ada's Laphroaig and revel with the poets. Aloud, as Clive insists.

Keep well and keep safe

With love

Elaine
28 September 2020

29
Vanity of Vanities!

Dear Friends,

Bill and I watched the American presidential debate last week. Oh dear. It was sad, so sad, to watch the embarrassment and diminution of a great nation. We've all read the commentary so there's nothing really to add except that I can't resist mentioning the brief letter to *The New York Times* from a woman who said simply, more or less, "Well, Melania's anti-bullying campaign's worked well on the home front, hasn't it?" And now that the coronavirus has muscled in on the whole sorry saga it has become a seriously worrying affair. Conspiracy theories abounding and worry upon worry about the outcome of the whole mess and what it means, not just for the US, but for the rest of the world. I think we're all reeling.

I don't wish to dismiss the serious nature of all this but I am going to confess that that debate was the first time I had watched President Trump for such a sustained period of time and my mind, searching desperately for sanity, was diverted by frivolity. Frivolity of a different kind. It's the hair thing. I found my eyes drawn by his coiffeur. The tan is bad enough but why at his age would you spend so much time and, indeed, money, on such a sweeping, sculptured bovver boy look.

My mind floated back to visions of a diplomat we once knew on one of our postings who was, shall we say, not young. His hair was puffed and preened and, dear God, pink! What was he thinking? Paul, one of our colleagues, and a man of great intelligence and wit, labelled it "a menopausal bouffant" and the term has stayed in our private lexicon. By the way, his wife was one of the most intimidating women I have ever met, hard as nails and hatchet-faced, with deeply-dyed black hair. Privately, playing fast and loose with the German, we called her Frau Kommandant, and I used to muse about whether she made him do the pink thing in the hope that an alleged youthful look on his part would make her look younger. That wouldn't have worked, I though bitchily; nothing would have achieved that, and I would ponder gleefully about their mixing up the dye bottles in the bathroom.

"Vanity of vanities, all is vanity", wrote that cynic and pessimist, the teacher in the Old Testament book of Ecclesiastes. I agree with him (given the times it probably was a man). It's all very well for me to make fun of the vanity of President Trump and others but I've had my own hair moment. It was at my ordination as priest in 1993. Obviously, it's a big thing and one is meant to have one's mind trained completely on higher things. A little context . . . There is a moment in the ceremony when the ordinand kneels before the bishop, who lays hands on the ordinand's head. Clergy gather around and you can feel their hands, shifting feathery touches on your shoulders, back, arms. You feel the bishop's hands on your head and hear the words: *Send down the Holy Spirit upon your servant, whom we set apart by the laying on of our hands, for the office and work of a priest in your Church.* Once upon a time, other words were added: *Whose sins thou dost forgive, they are forgiven: and whose sins thou dost retain, they are retained.*

They reek, these last words, of power conferred, of a right and capacity to do unto others many things, not all of them good. They're hard-edged, uncompromising and clear. All command and challenge and they have not always been used wisely but have sometimes been misused with all the malicious intent, or spite, or deliberate manipulation by the strong over the weak, of which humankind is capable. These last words were not used at my ordination but they lurked in the background, hovering among the organ pipes, swooping around trying to catch my eye. But any thought of them was wiped out by a reminder of ever present human fallibility. It was an extremely hot February day and, when I felt the bishop's hands on my head, a stray mundane thought chased any holy thoughts from my mind, "Oh, my God, I used hairspray!" A cartoon image popped into my mind of the bishop raising his hands and long strings of sticky goop hanging from his fingers to my hair. The thought and the image were gone in a moment but it was a sharp reminder that hubris always lurks to catch us out and humility is a hard-won thing.

A propos of humiliation, or more correctly, humility, I am reminded of an occasion when I was given a wonderful lesson in human grace and kindness. It was in Cairo—our first posting. I was young, oh so young, and trying terribly hard to get things right. We attended a reception to farewell a South American diplomat and his wife who were being transferred to Australia and I guess Bill was representing our ambassador. These days, give me fifteen minutes and I can be ready to venture forth and do the diplomatic polite but in those days of lingering teenage angst it took me hours. I had long hair and had been to the hairdresser to have some amazing confection of swirls and bangs and long side ringlets created and (of course) plastered into place with quantities of hairspray. Long dresses were high fashion at the time, which was great for me with my not particularly elegant flat shoes. I even remember the dress. Sleeveless (oh, for youth!), a low-necked buttoned top and a drawstring waist with a floating swirly skirt. Big pink flowers on a paler pink background. (Please no comments—I know!)

The car pulled up under the *porte cochère* from which rose a long flight of steps. I stepped out of the car and fell flat on my face. Look, I can't do elegant. When I fall getting up is a mess. It's all hands and feet and butt in the air. Trying desperately to get it all together I got up with Bill's help, gathered my skirts and set off up the stairs, thinking wistfully, "Please couldn't I just go home now!" We reached the top and I fell again, but this was worse. I slid on my stomach across the shiny slippery marble and came to a halt at the feet of the hostess, she standing with her husband to receive their guests.

I swear that woman was twelve feet tall. She dripped with a ransom of diamonds and glitter (and me in simple pearls). Besides, her gown reeked of Paris or Rome or Milan, unlike my made-in-Cairo by a modestly-priced tailor little pink number. Every seam and swathe shrieked Dior or Balenciaga or Valentino. Prone at her feet, I looked up and met her disdainful gaze and wanted to die. Right there. I wish I'd had the spirit to think something like "and then you'd have a mess to deal with, you stuck-up cow!" but I didn't. I just wanted to be somewhere else. Anywhere else.

Bill helped me to my feet (again, poor man!) and I did my best to greet our hosts as if nothing at all unusual had happened. Just as I was about to make my miserable way out of the Grand Presence, I felt a hand on my elbow and there was Mr Coorey. Sri Lankan

Ambassador. I didn't really know him except by sight (Bill was far too junior for us to mix with ambassadors very often) but there he was. He tucked my hand into his arm and gently led me away, saying, "Come with me, my dear. There are some people I would like you to meet." Dear wonderful Mr Coorey. It was a gift of great kindness to a young inexperienced girl from a man of dignity and grace. I loved Mr Coorey and he remains one of my heroes.

Heroes. I spoke of them last week and then we had the death of Australian singer Helen Reddy and an outburst of commentary saying things like "hero" and "feminist icon". It set me thinking. I knew her name, who she was and that she lived in the US. I knew there was a famous song, *I Am Woman*, and that she was much respected, but there was a gap between my memory and the press hyperbole. One of the things about diplomatic life is that you end up with gaps when you've missed things because, certainly in our early days, communications weren't all that swift. At one time no radio, at others no TV, and sometimes only weekly newspapers which trickled down through the embassy by rank. It was easy to miss things. Helen Reddy was big in the 70s, some of which years we spent in Canberra, but somehow she still didn't impinge much on my world. I asked my friend Sarah about her memories and they more or less matched mine: patchy. We decided that the fact that she achieved her success in America made the difference; perhaps being busy with children and having no money for buying extras like records and so on also played a part.

Whatever the reason, the words of her most famous song hit me last week as they obviously had many women before. "I am woman, hear me roar" rattled around in my brain. It became a week of reflection about what had been and what hadn't, what obstacles had not been overcome, what chances were missed, what risks hadn't been taken, what choices had been made, and what went wrong as a result. Sarah and I agreed that the best word for our feelings about all this is "rueful". And we smiled a little sadly, were realistic about the challenges piled up before women then (and often still are), and talked about the successes we had had despite all that. Might-have-beens never do anyone any good so we roared a little and felt comforted to have reached a time in life when hurts are somewhat dulled and there's still excitement and hope left.

Vale Helen Reddy.

Now we watch our children and know we didn't get everything wrong. We watch our grandchildren and know that the world they will live and work in will be nothing like ours, it will often be tougher, but their parents are preparing them well and the light of hope and excitement is bright for them as well.

I hope it gets better but currently this world seems hellbent on division rather than unity, on silencing difference rather than exploring it, on intolerance rather than acceptance. All of which will make things tougher for our grandchildren. There aren't too many signs of improvement right now. This thought reminded me of a snippet I'd written down some time and I rummaged around in fat files of bits and pieces I've kept for possible use till I tracked it down. A comment in a book called *On the Psychology of Military Incompetence*. I found it on our friend Andrew's bookshelf, he a priest and former army chaplain. The title sounded, well, unusual and therefore worth a browse. How ironic, I wonder, was the author, one Norman F. Dixon, being when he wrote:

> It is a feature of strongly held dogmas that they steadfastly resist not only unpalatable truths but even the faintest suggestion of the barest possibility of the most tangential reference to an unacceptable fact. Better that men should die and cities be overrun than that the sacred teaching should be found wanting.

Words for our times? Maybe we should ask "why pick on military incompetence only?" What about common old political incompetence?

Enough already. We gave a birthday dinner during the week for Philippa. The dress code was "posh frocks" which was great fun. The Dear knows what possessed me but I decided I would make chocolate ganache with crème fraîche, orange oil and spiced hazelnuts for dessert. Not too bright a decision because I was actually not all that well; over-anticipated recovery from a cold. Anyway, I ploughed ahead and explained to Bill that the ganache would be soft and spongey enough to be shaped into quenelles. In the event, it wasn't; the flavour was great but I had to slice it. Bill's comment? Terrific but he was sorry he hadn't been able to bring out the old line. A man had regretted the fact that quenelles always seemed to be served as a trio. He wanted one more so he could greet the dish saying, "Ah, wonderful! Four quenelles!"

What more can I say?

Keep well and keep safe

With love

Elaine
5 October 2020

30
O Saverio!

Dear Friends,

Yesterday we celebrated both our grandson Charlie's 20th birthday and what would have been my late father's 112th. Also our friend Robbie's birthday (further details top secret!). A superior date! Happy thoughts in sombre times.

Last March, Australia closed its borders even for most Australians planning travel in or out of the country. This has caused difficulties for lots of people who are still trying to return home, or make emergency family visits, for funerals, weddings, or tending ailing relatives. For the rest of us, it's meant all overseas trips cancelled for the whole year and who knows when we will be able to travel again. There have been, and still are, domestic travel restrictions as well so we've all become very familiar with our own particular four walls. When you can't travel, the memories that float to the surface are all palm trees and tropical sunsets, or crisp chardonnay in an alpine Shangri-La. But that's by no means the whole thing, as travel memories come flooding back to me . . . . . .

Traveling from Egypt to Cyprus decades ago and getting tested for amoebic dysentery (just the thing to do on a holiday), we encountered a doctor who told us eagerly he'd gone into stool testing . . . as a hobby! We left his office quickly, or at least as quickly as we could, when our 'business' was done . . . . . . Travelling in Nicaragua I managed to acquire Hepatitis A and typhoid at the same time. Bad move, people; don't ever do that one. So much for being vaccinated. A bright daffodil yellow and grounded for months, I got wonderfully thin but there are better ways of achieving that status . . . . . . Flying from New York to Sydney in the 1980s, I tangled with some dodgy seafood on the plane. Arrived in Sydney wanting to die immediately and not allowed to disembark because I'd also thrown up a bright red rash on my face. Eventually, staggering into the baggage claim area, I saw my suitcases going round and round on the conveyor belt, one of them open and my underwear displaying itself with no modesty at all before the world's vulgar gaze. The glamour of travel . . . . . .

Let me hasten to add that not all the trip disasters have been mine. A couple of years ago Bill returned from a work trip to Indonesia with a nasty case of pneumonia that landed him in hospital for five days. Bill's disasters have tended not to be illnesses but losses and of the what-were-you-thinking kind. As with the lost passports. He'd hidden them. Where? Umm. Frantic search ensued with my temper rising incrementally with each passing second until I heard a slightly rueful voice behind me. "Ah, yes, of course. Under the mattress." Under the mattress? We'd never done that before—or since. As I say, what was he thinking? That was in Connecticut, and I shouldn't have let him loose after that in case he lost himself. What he lost next was his reason! He'd seen a sign for a book sale and returned from a walk with nine or ten HEAVY books which we then had to lug through a six week trip. "But I had to," he wailed. "They were only $1 each!" Being a book obsessive myself, I understood, but bad timing, William. These particular purchases were all biographies of American political giants or analyses of American politics. Just what you want to read on a plane. (Speaking of politics, which I'm not going to, there was a good headline in *The Sydney Morning Herald* this week. An article about the President and the forthcoming US election under the clever byline 'Immaculate Infection'.)

Bill's really serious loss was Jumpy. This was a sweater I had knitted in 1975 (actually my sister Jane who is a serious knitter, as I am not, had to help because I got muddled up); Argyle pattern, plain grey with green diamonds. Very smart and he loved it. Over many years the jumper was reduced to home wear only (it needed patching here and there and, well, Bill changed shape a bit!) so I said he was not to wear it outside the house. Of course he did—to Fiji. Fiji? You need a sweater in the tropics? For the plane, I guess. He left it behind in his hotel. Hence frantic phone calls to the then Ambassador who, fortunately, was a good friend and set things in motion to rescue Jumpy. Anxious to hush this up, Bill begged the Minister he was accompanying, and whom we knew well, not to tell me or the consequences would be dire given Jumpy was subject to a travel ban. This minister, by the way, was with Bill and others once in Ephesus and managed a few free hours to tour the ruins. "What did they do in Ephesus?" one of the team asked. "They mostly received letters," was the Minister's dry reply.

Weird experiences (apart from that Cypriot doctor)? There've been quite a few. In Florence, a pair of Australian Christian missionaries from Melbourne tried to evangelise us after they heard our accents! "My husband's a lost cause," I said and we fled. A more usual memory of Florence was the statue of David; I managed to get a seat so I was able to spend time with him comfortably despite the gawking crowd around. "My, what big feet you have!" I thought.

For me possibly the most weird, or certainly the most unusual, travel experience was being taught to clean pigs' guts in Papua New Guinea. We were in Goroka in the Eastern Highlands staying with friends Meg and Daisy at Meg's coffee plantation. Their mother Yerema had presented them with an enormous pig for a feast. I sat through the ritualistic slaughter then some village women took me off in a pick-up truck to the local river. Fast-flowing and, I quickly discovered, freezing cold. The women hauled me through the waters to a rock in the middle and there I sat with them, washing the pig's intestines. This may not be an experience of much use in many diplomatic circles but, as cultural experiences go, it has given me serious bragging rights. We women did a lot of shrieking as we splashed through the icy waters and there was much hilarity as they watched me struggle with something at which they were greatly skilled. They plaited the intestines into ropes which then went into the earth oven with the meat and vegetables, and were destined for the women, allowing the men first go at the meat. How confronting such discrimination is.

Moving on from the weird and the wonderful I want to tell you about a favourite travel tale of mine. In Italy with our friend Peter, we moved to a villa we'd rented just outside a tiny Tuscan village. I say "villa" but it was quite an extensive estate. From the main house, the gardens stretched up a slope to another house with studio bedrooms and a fully equipped outside kitchen by a large swimming pool. Across the villa's wide lawns, at quite a distance, was a stable block, again with accommodations attached. All modern and in very good order. Gravelled driveways, rose gardens (I filled vases each morning—heaven!) and the whole establishment protected by high stone walls.

It was a mystery to me why such an extensive property was available for the modest rent we were paying. Perhaps because the main villa was not modern, with rather higgledy-piggledy levels, old-fashioned furniture with rather tired covers, not the most comfortable beds and an old-world kitchen with large refectory table, recalcitrant stove, ancient stone sink and a huge cast-iron chandelier which took real candles. I loved it.

One morning before we left for the day, I went to open the driveway gates and was startled by the sudden appearance in front of me of two rearing horses. My first glimpse was of a great black beast, wild-eyed and nostrils flaring, hooves it seemed inches from my face. Its rider slowly brought it under control. The horse quietened, the dust settled and the man leant down towards me, hand extended. I reached up to shake his hand, only to have it kissed instead. "I am Saverio," he said in deep tones, his eyes locked on mine. "I am the owner of the villa." My stomach flipped and fluttered. "Oh," I squeaked to myself. One hand held in his, the other floated to my face. Please let me find my voice, any voice, I pleaded silently. Girl, you are not a teenager any more. Act sophisticated. Don't trip on your own feet.

We chatted (sigh!), then Saverio kissed my hand again (eyes still holding mine) and galloped off. And, thinking I probably wouldn't wash my hand for at least that day, I made my way back into the house to tell Bill and Peter in an oh so nonchalant manner about my little adventure. And that was that. Off we went touring, me with a mind touching delicately now and again on how very nice it is to have one's hand kissed by a gallant stranger. Italian and French men know a thing or two and the sisterhood can eat their hearts out!

That evening, when we settled for a drink before dinner, Peter wandered in with a puzzled look on his face. He handed me a crested envelope saying, "This was tucked in the front gate. It says 'La Signora di Casa'". Opening it, I found a sheet of the villa's crested notepaper with a message in Italian. I nutted it out then said to the others, "Oh, isn't this nice! It's from Saverio, inviting me to come and visit his stables". Peter comes from a horsey family so I continued: "just think, Peter, you might get a mount!" It was then I heard a snort and turned to see Bill and Peter holding each other up, weak with suppressed laughter and tears running down their faces. I'd been set up! They'd gone online to get an Italian translation of this message, faked the handwriting and—I'd bought the whole thing! There really is nothing to do in such a situation but laugh and I knew this was a tale that would be told by those two—forever. And lo! it has come to pass. "O Saverio!" they like to say, rolling their eyes and chortling. Bastards. Mind you, I sometimes think "O Saverio!" a little fondly myself!

Back to reality and Canberra, this past week has upset my world in an irritating way. I have shingles. Memories (not good ones this time) of childhood chickenpox and the itch. The infuriating thing is that both of us have been vaccinated against shingles. I am now reminded that the vaccination does not guarantee complete protection, only about 50 to 60% safety. I guess this makes me one of the unlucky minority who succumb. I guess it also means getting vaccinated is a good idea; some protection is better than none. Go do it if you haven't already! I assure you, this is a very trying ailment though I'll spare you the details. Our friend Ada (of the wonderful smoked fish I've told you about) suggests I should call this letter 'Shit on Shingles' but I am studiously ignoring her.

Instead, I am minded to recall that Malcolm Guite sonnet *Because We Hunkered Down* I mentioned some weeks back. So many are still hunkered down; we in Canberra not much (forgetting my current self-imposed shingles isolation). Melbourne is still in lockdown; the US is still struggling; the UK is facing an upsurge in cases; India and Indonesia are in deep COVID-19 trouble. Figures in Australia are, and have been from the beginning of the pandemic, enviably low in comparison. "These bleak and freezing seasons may mean grace, when they are memory," Guite writes, but they are not memory yet. They will become our past, our history, "telling the story of our journey home". It's just that getting to the end of the journey is not that easy. One does not glide over muddy waters; one has to wade through them. But, Guite concludes his sonnet:

> Slowly, slowly, turning a cold key,
> Spring will unlock our hearts and set us free.

Hope is what one must cling to. And I see that sense of hope in the springtime awakening of our garden. In the little courtyard outside my study, the daphne has finished flowering but the miniature white clematis is in full and pretty bloom. In the main garden, roses are budding up for the summer, the Mexican sage bush hedge is a cloud of white flowers, the May bush and azaleas are about to burst. (Has anyone noticed my garden is essentially white?) The flower heads on the viburnum are growing and growing, green now, but soon to be white and the tree will be burdened with the weight of its lovely snowball flowers.

And very soon it will be Advent, that season of waiting and hopefulness that leads to Christmas. For us in the southern hemisphere, the traditional Christian metaphors often don't match our climate. Because most Australian trees are evergreen I did not fully appreciate the sharpness of the distinctions between life and death, summer fecundity and winter barrenness, until I experienced a northern hemisphere spring. Easter's metaphor of new life suits that northern spring and the bursting forth of fruit and flowers but comes for us as we descend into winter cold.

But Advent is exactly the right season for this moment for all of us. Even for you in northern climes. We wait and we hope for better times. This has very much been the case this year for Louise and Minik, separated for most of the year by the pandemic but now, in Copenhagen, they will be married on October 17. And, if all goes well, they will have a second wedding ceremony here in Canberra next year. Meanwhile, for Carol and Peter in New York, forced to put their wedding plans on hold last April, for them too all will be well. A new dawn for which they wait will bring for them also the beginning of a new adventure.

I began with travel, let me finish there. My adult life, at least forty-odd years with Bill in diplomatic service, from Cairo to Jakarta, has largely been bookended by the haunting Moslem call to prayer. In Egypt I learned to love it. A *muezzin's* cry is like a soul yearning for its god; it is a lilting love call floating from mosques to Allah and reminding the faithful to pause, remember, and honour their god. I came to enjoy Cairo days punctuated by the voice of faith even though faith was no part of my life then. "Allahu Akbar," Moslems say. "God is great," Jews and Christians say. For me, there is a special completeness in my journey from faithlessness to priesthood embraced by these calls.

But for this moment in all our lives, Malcolm Guite again:

> These bleak and freezing seasons may mean grace
> When they are memory . . .

Slowly, slowly, turning a cold key,
Spring will unlock our hearts and set us free.

Dear Friends, peace, spring grace and hope, be with you all.

Keep well and keep safe

With love

Elaine
12 October 2020

Lightning Source UK Ltd.
Milton Keynes UK
UKHW011901161220
375374UK00001B/44

9 781925 679885